GOD WITHIN US

John Wijngaards, theologian, scripture scholar and writer, spent his childhood in Indonesia and much of his working life in India. He "dabbled" in Chinese, studied Arabic for many years, and learnt Sanskrit and Telugu from Brahmin teachers. He was a board member of the Institute of Islamic Studies at Hyderabad. As Director of Amruthavani, a Telugu communication centre, he initiated the Dharma Vijayamu campaign that seeks to enlist the co-operation of adherents of all creeds to ensure the "victory of justice". He has written many books, including *Mukti Margam*, an explanation of Christian faith through (mainly Indian) stories, *The Breath that is Me*, *Inheriting the Master's Cloak* and *The Seven Circles of Prayer*. At present he heads Housetop Centre, London.

John Wijngaards

GOD WITHIN US

TEMPLEGATE PUBLISHERS
SPRINGFIELD, ILLINOIS

First published in Great Britain by
Collins Publishers

Published in the United States of America in 1990 by
Templegate Publishers
302 East Adams
P.O. Box 5152
Springfield, Illinois 62705 *2/96*

Manufactured in the United States of America

ISBN: 0-87243-177-0

Library of Congress Catalog Card Number: 89-51797

BT
102
.W54
1988
c.1

CONTENTS

Preface   Seeing God Upside Down   7

PART 1   *The Creator Within Us*

1 Grandfather's Clock and Cosmic Alarm 15
2 Turtle-Shells and Deep Water   21
3 The Creative Void of a Hunchback
   Tree   29
4 Horizons Unknown to a Frog in a Well 37
5 Faces Modelled Inside Out   43
6 The Way in to the Creator   51

PART 2   *The Inner Judge*

7 Big Brother's Watchful Eye   57
8 Layer upon Layer of Radiance   65
9 The Ant, the Stone, and the Pitchdark
   Night   73
10 The Mirror and the Lens Inside Us   80
11 The Way in to the Judge   89

PART 3   *Rescuing God From Our Thinking*

12 Sparks from the Mind's Furnace   95
13 The Power Perception of Ancient
   Myths   104
14 Deep but Dry-as-Dust Deductions   115
15 The Search for a Phantom Gardener   126

16   Prayer in the Stock Exchange   135
17   The Way in to "Grasping" God   146

PART 4   *The Musician In Our Heart*

18   He Pitches His Tent next door to Us   155
19   His Spirit Flows in Our Veins   164
20   The Way in to Love   170

Notes   176

PREFACE

Seeing God Upside Down

Many people, I am convinced, have a wrong idea of God. They speak of him as if he were the big Outsider. They fear him as if he were an opponent. They think of him as a force external to themselves. They do not realize that God is inside themselves, that they can find him or her within.

In 1973, when I was still lecturing at Hyderabad in India, I saw a Telegu film entitled *Adiparāshakti*, "the original divine energy". The film was not a great piece of art. It was a mythological production, pathetic, if not hilarious in some scenes. Vishnu, Shiva and Brahma, the three principal gods, were having a row with their wives, the goddesses Parvathy, Lakshmi and Saraswathy. Tempers ran high. Abuse was hurled at all and sundry. Heaven shuddered at the mutual threats uttered by the male and female divinities. Then the goddesses walked out; and appealed to the origin of all divinity, to *Adiparāshakti*, the original divine energy – who turned out to be female herself! Predictably she took the side of her sex. Adi withdrew divine power from the male gods. It reduced them to a laughable state of helplessness. As usual, woman power won.

I recall this film because it occasioned in me a new way of thinking about God. I have never been greatly impressed by the Hindu pantheon of gods, and I found the petty divine quarrelling depicted in the film as ridiculous a spectacle as I have ever watched. Yet there was something deep that got hold of me. It struck me that divine energy can come from *within* as well as from without. I had been vaguely aware of it, of course, through previous reading, but the implications of this insight all of a sudden overwhelmed me. I realized that I was turning God inside out. It fascinated me and frightened me. Various lines of enquiry I had pursued seemed to meet in one point. Suspicions and vague ideas began to fall into place. In short, something was happening to me that would make a great difference to my way of experiencing God.

Many years have passed since then and I have had plenty of time to grow, mature and be confirmed in my new approach to God. In this book I will attempt to share my findings. I hope that others may be helped the way I was. My message will be simple: Try to find God within you. He is closer to you and deeper in you than your conscious self.

It may be good if from the beginning I declare some of my principles. I am a convinced Christian, in fact a Roman Catholic priest. But I do not for a moment on that account reject the validity of other religious traditions. On the contrary, I greatly esteem all the major contributions to religious human experience. From my early student days I collected and avidly read the great classics of all ages: the Vedas, the Upanishads, the Tao Te Ching, the Dammapada, the Koran; and the writings of innumerable thinkers and mystics. I have never considered them alien to myself. For me they constitute a spiritual ancestry for the whole of humankind. These ancient writings are all part of a wider "Old Testament". They are the precious foundation on which my present belief rests.

I am also firmly convinced that the scientific method has brought untold benefit to our world. I am full of admiration for the achievements of technology, medicine, nuclear physics and microbiology. I am spellbound when reading reports on astronomy, archaeology or any other science. I have no doubt at all regarding evolution; I cringe when I hear people defend creationism in the name of religion. Truth is more fundamental to me than any preconceived religious notion.

When I say that we have to find God within, I do not for a moment mean that we ourselves *are* God, in some kind of pantheistic sense. God is Infinite, Absolute; beyond the limits of space and time. He (or she) is also the profoundest mystery that exists; incomprehensible because his (or her) reality transcends human words and images. To put ourselves on a par with this Source of all reality (by claiming we *are* God) would constitute the height of folly. But I do maintain that we are closer to this Source than most people are aware of. And we reach him (or her) most easily when we travel inwards.

Historical research has shown that there are two distinct and contrary patterns of religious experience. In so-called *prophetic* religious experience the way to God comes through a word of revelation. God is encountered as a Person who speaks and acts. He is the Other, the Thou, the one who faces us as a caring Father. In *centring* religious experience God is discovered in oneself. The way to God leads through images and symbols to forms of mystical participation. God meets us as the principle of ultimate unity, as our deepest Self, as the Mother. In Christianity itself both patterns have been present. Through the course of the centuries either the one or the other has been predominant in people's spirituality.[1] I believe that for myself and, perhaps, many

9

others like me, the inward approach is most helpful and liberating.

I am confirmed in this view by a recent study on *God in Europe*.[2] It shows that a majority believe in God (seventy-five per cent) though many feel ill at ease with traditional terminology about God. Only half of those who believe in God see him as a Person. The other half prefer to call him a Supreme Being, a Spirit, a Life Force. This does not necessarily imply a watering down of belief in God, as some commentators contend. Rather, says Dr J. Kerkhofs, the author of the study, we may be witnessing in Europe a shift from a more transcendent concept of divinity (God above us) to a more immanent one (God within us). This, I believe, is exactly what is happening, and through this book I want to validate and encourage this inward search.

It is not always a good idea to announce items on the menu before they are served up. Readers generally like to be kept in suspense as they turn from one chapter to the next — even if the book is not an adventure story or a who-dun-it. So I am not going to give away secrets or spoil surprises. I hope you will find it as exciting to read my ramblings as I found it to write them — which, I suppose, is a tall order.

I must warn you that not all sections of the book play the same role. In fact, they may be compared to different rooms in my house. Parts one and two (on God as Creator and Judge) are for every-day living; they represent my bedroom and my sitting room. Part three (on God's being trapped in human thought) is more academic. It finds its equivalent in my study, with its bookshelves and encyclopedias. Some readers may find the going tough here — and will skip the pleasure of sharing my skirmishes with learned philosophers. Part four (on God as Lover) corresponds to my prayer room. I realize that few people nowadays have prayer rooms in their homes. I have. I invite you to enter my sanctuary and exchange religious experiences as we sit crosslegged on the floor. I conclude every part with a "Way In" chapter with practical and down-to-earth suggestions. Look on them as windows that let in fresh air and afford views in various directions.

Talking about my way with God is very much like allowing strangers to invade my personal living space; an embarrassing thought when I look around me: crumbs on my carpet, piles of unwashed dishes in my sink, files and papers littering every available tabletop. The last thing I would want to do is to present my house as a model for the Ideal Home Exhibition! Even less should I presume to offer my experience of God as exemplary or unique.

It is precisely the accessibility and simplicity of my discovery that makes my message cogent, I feel. If my living space, common to a fault, could be so transformed by my new awareness of God, the same experience lies within reach of all.

PART ONE

THE CREATOR
WITHIN US

1

Grandfather's Clock and Cosmic Alarm

"Suppose you walk through a park," my religion teacher once said in class, "and you see a blanket spread out on the grass, with a picnic basket on it, sandwiches, apples and a tin of Coca-Cola. Even if you see nobody around, you know they were put there by a human person. A blanket can't walk. A basket can't carry itself. In the same way, when we look at the universe, we know it was created by Someone outside it. Nothing in the universe can make itself: neither a stone, nor the earth, nor the stars, nor a whole galaxy. Everything finite that exists must owe its existence to an infinite, self-sufficient Being. Sheer logic compels us to accept an eternal, omnipotent, unlimited Creator."

The argument, even if it has its validity, evokes an image of God as craftsman and organizer. Because *we* produce artefacts by selecting different kinds of material and putting them together in a new structural order, we think of God as having done the same. Of course, he does surpass us by his power and skill, that we grant—he created the materials he needed out of nothing, and combined them in ways infinitely more ingenious and imaginative than we could have done. All the same, creation was a *job*, a piece

15

of craftsmanship, the work of an organizer. This is also how the first chapter of the Bible describes creation.

God collected basic materials by his repeated command: "Let there be . . . !" The ingredients for his manufacturing process were light, land, a sky, plants, fish, cattle and so on. Then he put everything in its place. The sun and the moon were suspended from the sky to divide day and night. Dry land was separated from the sea. Fishes were let loose in the water, birds in the air. The land was furnished with plants and animals. The Bible thus presents the world as a house which God the master architect, built for the human race.

Philo of Alexandria (20 B.C. – A.D. 54) was a Jew who knew the Genesis account well. As philosopher and writer he had also studied Aristotle's arguments. For him the conclusion that God is the ultimate craftsman followed from the nature of the world itself. "When we come across a statue or painting, do we not form at once an idea of the sculptor or painter? When we inspect a dress, a ship or a house, do we not immediately conceive a notion of the weaver, or shipbuilder, or architect who made them?" So God's identity too, he concludes, could be established from the universe. "No artificial product can exist of its own accord. The world is the most artificial and skilfully made of all products. Therefore it carries the mark of having been put together by some extremely skilled person, someone most perfect in knowledge[3]".

Now I do not want here to enter into the argument itself, its mythopoic origins or its function in philosophy. I want to reflect on *the image* it evokes, an image that was bound to make God far and distant.

In the Middle Ages the world, as people knew it, was incredibly small. The earth was still believed to be a flat disk, about the size of Europe. The sky was like a huge dome, with the sun and the stars gliding along it almost

16

within human reach. Travel being as slow as it was, the distances in the known world were large enough to impress people; yet from another point of view the "ends of the earth" were reasonably near. God, enthroned in his heavenly palace just above the sky, could be imagined to keep everything under close surveillance.

For God was thought to be directly involved in everything that went on in his creation. The sun, the moon and the stars were pushed along by angels specially appointed to that task. The weather belonged to God's own portfolio, and he guided the seasons from month to month. At times he might send a frost or a drought to punish a sinful nation; then their repentance and insistent pleas might make him relent so as to avert total disaster. Every single human being owed his or her life to God's specific decision to infuse a human soul into the embryo. Everything important that happened to an individual came directly from God's hand: health or sickness, failure or good fortune, one's marriage partner, one's children, the moment of death. God was terribly close, for not only was he the creator, he was imagined to be like a puppet master holding every creature on a string.

This image of God was bound to shatter into a thousand pieces with the increase of our knowledge of the universe. We realize now that our earth is but a speck in an immensely vast system of millions of galaxies and clusters of galaxies. Some of the light we capture in our telescopes has travelled twelve billion light years to reach us – a distance completely beyond our imagination, if we remember that light covers 300,000 km in just one second! Since the traditional image placed God *outside* the universe, he was pushed further and further away with every new awareness of cosmic size.

God's direct causality in every-day events underwent a similar fate. In every sphere of science God's intervention was shown to be unnecessary. The weather, for instance,

17

is entirely dominated by natural forces: the turning of the globe, the processing of the sun, currents of water and air caused by variations in temperature and pressure. Life too holds no secrets. The origin of a child can be followed from the moment of conception, the formation of the first cell by the cohesion of the father's and mother's chromosomes, to delivery and birth. Disease, we know, is due to natural disorders: to microbes, viruses, cancer or malnutrition. God, the puppet master, the stage manager, the organizer, seems no longer to be required to explain the events that touch us more directly. In this respect too he has been pushed away out of our view.

The larger the universe is and the more complicated in its structure, the more it requires a creator, religious people will tell us. Right. But what we are discussing now is *the image* of God as the outside creator. That image, whatever our philosophical reasonings may tell us, has let us down, for God has become so far and distant as to be virtually non-existent. There is the famous story of the astronomer Laplace who had constructed a replica of the solar system according to Newtonian principles. It showed the earth and the planets rotating round the sun like a giant clock. When Laplace showed his contraption to Napoleon Bonaparte, the latter is supposed to have asked: "And where does Almighty God fit into the picture?" "I've no longer any need of that hypothesis", Laplace replied. God the clockmaker, clockwinder, clockmender has disappeared from our world.

It is a hilarious thing to say, but we have organized our own life so adequately that we feel quite self-sufficient. We live in houses built by ourselves. All the furniture is fabricated. We use water, gas and electricity generated by our industries. We buy food and clothes in supermarkets. When we venture outside we travel on paved streets in cars or buses. We surround ourselves with radio and

18

television sets, calculators and word processors. We manage our own lives, we think, through science and technology. God is dead, as far as we are concerned.

Of course, it does not really work. We are fragile human beings, and all the apparatus of urbanized living cannot save us from being such. We want to know what the meaning of life really is. We discover that money and technology cannot actually make us happy, in spite of all the comfort they produce. We are suddenly confronted with the mystery of existence by an unexpected death. We love to leave our steel-and-stone fortresses and roam in a forest, or walk along a beach, or climb the face of a mountain. We know there are dimensions in us that can never be satisfied by mathematics and machines. We are beings with emotion, with a mind that searches deeper than matter, with a self-awareness that cries for affirmation. The old questions which the God-creator faith sought to answer, still need a reply.

Does the solution not stare us in the face? I have said already that we cannot run away from ourselves. God has become so far removed from us because we approached him as a creator *outside* us. But suppose he is just the opposite? Suppose he is more accurately described as the deepest source within us, the source from which we sprang forth? Suppose he is the inner presence in everything we are and everything we see? The image of an architect, a carpenter, a clockmaker fails precisely because such craftsmen leave their products behind. Once they have done their job, they can walk away, and the objects they have produced continue on their own. But suppose we are related to God in a different way? Suppose we *are* the architect, the carpenter, the clockmaker to the extent God manifests himself in us?

Adjusting ourselves to this new image of creation requires time. We are so used to the "outside creator" image that it has become a prejudice. And prejudices are frames of

19

reference that are charged with emotion, we cannot abandon them overnight. Someone I knew called Jim had a comparable experience when his father married a second time.

The woman Jim's father married was one of Jim's colleagues in the office. From being a friend and companion whom he used to tease and cheer up, she had suddenly become his step-mother! It took some time before Jim had made all the mental and emotional readjustments required by the new situation. We too need time to sit back so that we can digest the implications of an inverted creator image.

I can think of no better way of doing this than by introducing some ancient spiritual masters, the Taoists, who believed in an internal creator. If we take the trouble to see the world as they saw it, we will begin to understand the implications of our new approach to God. If God is the source of all we are, as the inner well of being and energy within us, we will discover a new focus. Could it be that the noise of hard work, production and organization prevents us from finding God? Could it be that silence reveals him?

2

Turtle-Shells
and Deep Water

In daily life we can be so preoccupied with external things that we do not live but are "being lived". We do not walk; we run. Our eyes strain under an endless stream of images: streets, walls, faces, newspapers, television. Our ears take in the continuous noise of screeching traffic, prattling talk, pulsating music. We are under pressure. We have to succeed. We are meeting minimum standards and deadlines. Competition impels us forward; so does the clock. Hardworking achievers as we are, we drive ourselves on. Then, in the evening, flushed and fatigued by the day's activity, we get drunk on newsy thrills or intoxicating fiction – till we pass out. And this we call living.

Lao Tzu recorded a warning in his *Tao Te Ching*:

> Block your mouth,
> shut the doors of eyes and ears,
> and you will have fullness within.
> Open your mouth,
> be always busy,
> and you're beyond hope![4]

Instinctively we may feel that he is offering valuable advice.

21

Yes, we have to stop running. We have to guard our senses; or we will run dry. But what exactly did the ancient Chinese master mean? Was he talking about the same problems that afflict us today? How, in fact, can we presume that someone who lived twenty-three centuries ago, and in a country so far removed from our own, has anything sensible to say to people who live here and now?

I believe the original Taoist thinkers should be listened to for two reasons. First, they reacted to social conditions that were not so different from our own, as I will presently explain. Secondly, in formulating a solution they drew on their own deep mystical insights; so that the truths they expressed retain lasting validity. A ruby set in a gold ring may have been fashioned for a princess whose name is forgotten; it retains its beauty because the quality of its material and the skill of its craftsmanship do not diminish with time.

When presenting Taoist thought in this and the next two chapters, I want to avoid the kind of academic discussion that would distract. For simplicity's sake I will take for granted that the *Tao Te Ching* was written by the legendary Lao Tzu[5] and the *Nan Hua Chen Ching* by Chuang Tzu.[6] Even if some chapters were added later by disciples, they reflect the teaching of the masters. Then there is the question of which version to use. Chinese idiom is short and pointed, but often hard to render in clear English. When quoting original passages I will offer my own free translation, which will be partly based on the more literal, classical versions available, and partly on my own interpretation in the light of context and commentary. Being faithful to the mind of Chinese teachers requires more than literal renderings. It calls for a dynamic interpretation that makes sense to twentieth-century seekers.

The Taoists arose during one of the most confusing

political eras in Chinese history, the "Warring States" period (475–221 B.C.). For China it was a time of painful growth. Agriculture was intensified. New crops were introduced. Fertilizers were imported. Irrigation schemes became commonplace. Towns and cities sprang up, to serve both as fortresses and trade centres. Silk, lacquer, silver ornaments and other luxury goods changed hands as eagerly as wheat, rice and wool. The iron industry, based on locally invented blast furnaces, produced high quality tools and weapons. A more relaxed feudal system of government was replaced by centralized monarchies. The new kings surrounded themselves with civil servants to tax the farmers. They raised professional armies to defend the land against enemies. For in this period of rapid change everyone was enemy of almost anyone else. Thirteen larger and smaller states were continuously in conflict with each other. The wars which thrived on the insatiable greed and ambition of kings, chancellors and generals, could never lead to lasting peace.

This was the chaos Chuang Tzu came to know so well as a minor official at Ch'i-Yuan in his home state of Meng. If we are to believe tradition, he left his post, withdrew to the countryside and turned philosopher, giving advice to whoever came to consult him. Soon his reputation grew, and the king of the neighbouring state of Ch'u decided to enlist his services. He despatched two envoys with a letter that stated: "Hereby I appoint you my chancellor." The envoys delivered the message to Chuang Tzu as he stood knee-deep in Pu river, fishing with a bamboo pole.

Still holding his pole and looking speculatively at Pu river, Chuang Tzu said: "I believe there is a sacred turtle, offered and canonized three thousand years ago, which is worshipped by the king. Wrapped in silk it lies in a precious shrine on an altar in the temple. What do you think: If you were a turtle, would you prefer to lose your life and leave your dead shell to be an object of worship shrouded in incense for three thousand years? Or would you prefer to live as a plain turtle that drags its tail in the mud?"

"For the turtle", said the envoy, "it might be better to stay alive and drag its tail in the mud!"

"Precisely", Chuang Tzu replied. "Go home. Leave me here to drag my tail in the mud."[7]

It is not difficult to see that Chuang Tzu is speaking of plain survival. Prime ministers led conspicuously short lives in those days, and few came unscathed through the incessant bloody court intrigues. A king might overwhelm an official with favours one day; and then cheerfully chop off the man's toes the next, at the request of one of his consorts. Some commentators therefore see the main point of Chuang Tzu's reply in escape from entanglement and death—Taoist wisdom aimed at physical survival in turbulent times, they contend.

Survival yes, but then of a special kind. Let us look at the story again. Chuang Tzu was put before a vital decision. Any normal Chinese of that time would have wondered what the most auspicious course to follow would be. And here the turtle comes into the picture. Turtle-shells were the favourite tool of divination in those days. It was thought that each turtle represented heaven and earth in his shell: the vaulted sky in its carapace or upper shell; the earth in its lower shell. After killing and sacrificing the turtle, its shell would be placed on a fire. From the cracks in its lower shell favourable or unfavourable omens could be read. In fact, it is almost certain that the sacred shell in the royal shrine referred to by Chuang Tzu, was precisely a shell venerated and preserved by the monarch because it was believed to confirm the accession of his dynasty. Sometimes the diviner's interpretation was engraved on the shell next to the tell-tale cracks. Such engravings on tortoise-shells commissioned by the Shong dynasty (18th–12th centuries B.C.) are the earliest known Chinese ideographs we possess. In short, no one would have been surprised if Chuang Tzu had caught a turtle to find out what divine counsel could be found on its shell.

The real Taoist "twist" is that Chuang Tzu "reads" the turtle in a new way. There lies a mystery in the turtle, as even diviners admitted. We read in *Kuan-yin-tzu*: "The turtle-shell has no Self and yet it has knowledge of great matters."[8] And the *I Ching* declares: "To unravel complex matters, to search out what is hidden, to bring up what lies deep and reach out to what is far, thereby discerning good from evil among all events under the sky . . . there are no more potent means than yarrow stalks and the turtle-shell."[9] Chuang Tzu agrees with the mystery, but sees it on a deeper level. The turtle carries a divine answer in itself, though not as markings on its shell. It carries it, like any other being, in the mysterious principle that causes it to be and that gives it life.

For the turtle is a remarkable animal. It is hard and soft at the same time. It waddles on land but swims nimbly under water. It has serious eyes and a funny tail. When threatened it pulls in all its limbs and lies rigid as a stone. But when it moves in its own space, in the muddy water of the river, it darts along, happy and agile. The lesson of the turtle is that it can only grow and be happy in its natural surroundings. How does this apply to human beings? Where is our "space", our natural surrounding? Do we find it in competition, warfare, ambitious production? Do we obtain it by victory, power, wealth? Or does it lie on a deeper plane – when we discover what it means to be human?

Fish thrive in water;
human beings thrive in Tao.
Water animals seek the deep shadow of the pool

and satisfy their needs.
If human beings who thrive in Tao
immerse themselves
in non-action,
their nature is realized.
The lesson is:
Fish need to lose themselves
in rivers and lakes,
people in the practice of Tao.[10]

In this text we meet for the first time the expressions "Tao" and "non-action". I will explain them more fully in the next two chapters. Here it may suffice for us to notice that they denote *inner* realities. It is characteristic for human beings to be happy when we open ourselves to such *spiritual* dimensions. Though external involvement is necessary and fruitful, as we shall see later, it only makes sense if we have first discovered depth and truth in ourselves. The Taoists did not preach escape – though we can hardly blame them for wanting to be spared the hassle of unchecked ambition or the risks of senseless warfare. What they advocated was the return to deeper waters where the human spirit could discover its own worth. In practical terms this meant: withdrawing from external noise and diving into silence.

"Our mind benefits greatly from peace and stillness. Do not fret, do not allow yourself to be upset and the experience of deep harmony will come, of its own accord. It is close at hand, standing at the door; yet is intangible, outside our conscious control. It may seem as distant as the furthest limit of the universe; yet it is not far off. Every day we use its power. For Tao fills us completely but we cannot pin it down. It leaves us, yet has not departed. It arrives and is not around. It is silent, producing no sound that can be heard; but suddenly it is present in the mind. It

26

is hazy and dark, has no distinct contours, yet in a great stream it flowed into us at birth."[11]

To combat noise, our chief enemy, we should first of all temper the inner turmoil of our thoughts and words. Why do we talk so much? The *Tao Te Ching* points out how hollow and shallow talk can be.

Honest words are not beautiful;
beautiful words are not honest. (c.81)

The more words, the less they count. (c.5)

Don't boast or brag.
Who strides cannot maintain the pace. (c.24)

Who knows does not speak;
who speaks doesn't know. (c.56)

Talking little is only natural.
Gusty winds don't last all morning;
downpours cannot last all day. (c.23)

A truly wise person is not a chatterbox. The best guide teaches without words (c.43). The master instructs his disciples in non-talking (c.2). Only thus can the Tao be found.

In order to become aware of this interior source of energy we have to make space for silence. We must refuse to be deafened by noise all day or to be totally immersed in external activity. In practical terms this involves consciously seeking silence from time to time. The Taoists called this *tso-wang*, sitting with an empty mind. By a cessation of outside impressions and the withdrawal of the senses to an interior point of focus, calm and quiet may be found. Silence functions as healing. Our soul has, as

27

it were, been silted up by successive deposits of talk, work and trouble. Travelling back through these layers of external consciousness, we have to "return to stillness". It is in the point of original stillness that we discover our true self, says the *Tao Te Ching*.

The heavy underlies lightness.
The still overcomes unrest. (c.26)

Empty yourself of everything.
Let your mind hold to stillness.
The ten thousand things rise and fall
while the Self watches their return.
They teem and flourish,
then return to the source.
Returning to the source is stillness
which is the way of nature. (c.16)

Movement generates heat,
but stillness overcomes it.
Stillness and tranquillity
set things in order in the universe. (c.45)

By adopting stillness we can learn to see with new eyes. We drift like the waves of the sea (c.20) ready to be guided. We become receptive like a hollow cave (c.15). We are as open and flexible as a little child with no prejudice (c.49). We return to the state of an uncarved block of wood (c.28).

These were the kind of things that went through Chuang Tzu's mind as he stood fishing in Pu river. How could he ever exchange the experience of inner stillness with the noise and turmoil of a job at court! Rather, like the turtle seeking deep water, would he plunge himself in an encounter with Tao. What that means we will see in the next chapter.

3

The Creative Void
of a Hunchback Tree

With even a little experience of life we know that things are often not what they seem. A Taoist would go further. "Things are *never* what they seem", he would tell us. "There is success in failure and failure in success. Beautiful things are ugly and ugly things are beautiful. For failure and success are but two sides of one coin. Beauty withers and ugliness turns into beauty. Everything changes; except for the immutable reality, Tao, which underlies both failure and success, beauty and squalor."

A story may illustrate the point. A carpenter called Shih was on his way to the state of Chi accompanied by an apprentice. When they arrived at Chu Yuan they rested under a huge oak tree that overshadowed the village shrine. The tree spread a wide canopy of branches and towered as high as a hill. The apprentice was impressed. "Master," he exclaimed, "never since I took up my axe and followed you, have I set eyes on more tempting timber. Why don't you even look at it?"

"Shut up!", Shih replied. "This tree is useless. The branches are gnarled and twisted; they won't do for beams or rafters. The trunk is curved and knotted; it can't be used for coffins. Look at its wood: it's all worthless timber.

A boat made of it would sink, a coffin would rot, a tool would split, a door would ooze sap and a beam would have woodworm. That's why it has been left alone, because it's useless."

That night the sacred oak appeared to Shih in a dream. "Why are you belittling me?", it cried. "Are you comparing me to so called useful trees? Have you never noticed what happens to them? Apple, pear, orange and other fruit trees are stripped bare at harvest. They are pruned or cut down when they don't produce; all because they are 'useful'. And what about catalpa, cypress and mulberry trees? As soon as they reach maturity, they are sawn into planks, beams and boards. You see, if you're useful you attract attention. I've been trying for a long time to be useless. Once or twice an axe was laid to me, but being useless saved me. Could I ever have grown so large, if I had been useful?"

When the carpenter remained speechless, the oak continued with even greater scorn. "You and I are both things. How can one thing presume to judge another thing? What does a fallible and useless man like you know about a useless tree?"

Shih woke up and began to reflect on the meaning of his dream. When he narrated the dream to his apprentice, the latter said: "If the oak really wants to be useless, why does it overshadow the shrine?"

"By golly! You are right", Shih exclaimed. "It's only pretending to be useless. No one will dare to cut it down because it is a sacred tree. That's how it protects itself. We must look at it from a different point of view."[12]

The story deliberately baffles us. A giant tree proves to be useless. We then realize how useful this uselessness is. Finally we discover it has some use, after all. The point is not only to make us discover that everything is relative; that much depends on the angle from which we view things.

30

The Taoist master wants us to feel the "swing" from one extreme to the other; as from usefulness to uselessness, and vice versa.

For life is an endless chain of such "swings". The one undeniable observation we cannot miss is that everything we know changes: from life to death, and from death to life; from fame to disrepute, and from disrepute to fame; from weakness to power, and from power to weakness. An insignificant seed grows to be a strong tree, then succumbs to the axe. A promising sapling is struck by lightning but turns out to outlive all other trees in its patch of forest.

The Taoists loved the image of the gnarled and useless tree. For them it was a frozen symbol of change – and thus capable of pointing to the permanent reality underlying all change. Suppose some sacrificial bowls are carved from an old tree. The bowls are painted with green and yellow designs. The splinters of wood that have been cut away lie rotting in a ditch. One part of the tree has become a piece of art, the other part trash. But are they really different? Were they not both part of the natural tree? Our senses deceive us. Fingering the bowl we love its touch, we admire the colours, we smell the perfume it contains and we like the sound when we tap its sides. Thus we are taken in and fail to see the original nature of the wood.[13]

The tree has become a parable. It teaches us that we should look underneath realities that change. What we find there is Tao. "Life is followed by death; death is followed by life. What cannot be done, can be done; what can be done, can no longer be done. Right becomes wrong and wrong right. The flow of life changes circumstances and then things themselves are changed in turn . . . People will never see Tao when they only notice one of a pair of opposites, when they concentrate on only one aspect of being . . . The pivot of Tao passes through the centre where

31

all affirmations and denials converge. He who holds to the centre is at the still-point from which all change and all opposition can be seen in its right perspective."[14]

Looking at the transformations of a gnarled tree we become aware of Tao. Tao is the unchanging "whole" of which all limited things are temporary expressions. When we become aware of Tao, all becomes relative. "When we look at things in the light of Tao, there is no 'better' or 'worse'. Everything is good and can be considered 'better' than something else, seen on its own terms. Everything is greater than one thing and smaller than another. The whole world is a grain of rice. The tip of a hair is as large as a mountain."[15] Unbelievable though it may seem, in one useless old tree we may suddenly glimpse the core of the universe.

For Tao is the absolute reality that produced all the things we see. "The Tao begot one. One begot two. Two begot three. And three begot the ten thousand things."[16] The One is the Tao itself, looked at as unifying principle. The two are heaven and earth, or yin and yang, the pair of opposites. The ten thousand things comprise all changing creatures. Tao made everything to be what it is. It created from within the most various beings.

> From the beginning, these things arose from the One:
> Heaven is clear through the One.
> The earth is solid through the One.
> The spirits have power through the One.
> The valley produces plenty through the One.
> The ten thousand things have life by the One.
> Kings and lords rule the country through the One.
> It is the One that makes them what they are.[17]

The Tao is, therefore, the inner life force that brings forth, causes to be, supports. The Tao is inescapable. It is the bedrock of existence. It is the foundation, the source, the root. Things are what they are because of it. "The Tao is that from which one cannot deviate. That from which one can deviate is not the Tao."[18] "The Tao causes life and death; losing it people die, gaining it they live. Whatever is done without Tao fails; whatever is done through Tao succeeds. Tao has no roots, no stem, no leaves, no blossom. And yet the birth and growth of the ten thousand things, each according to its kind, depend on Tao."[19]

What more can we say about Tao? Very little, because words fail. Human language uses nouns and names to distinguish specific objects. But the characteristic of Tao is precisely that it is not specific. It does not carry any of the limiting traits that apply to the creatures it produces.

The Tao that can be put into words
     is not the eternal Tao.
The name that can be named
     is not the everlasting name,[20]

It cannot be seen – it is beyond form.
It cannot be heard – it is beyond sound.
It cannot be held – it is intangible . . .
Hard to observe, it cannot be named.
It fades into nothingness
as the shape of the shapeless
as the image of the imageless;
indefinable, beyond imagination.[21]

A reality mysteriously formed,
complete before heaven and earth,
silent and void,
standing on its own and unchanging,
ever present, never outdone:

33

it can be the mother of the ten thousand things.
I do not know its name;
therefore I call it "Tao".[22]

Some Western scholars are at pains to point out that the
Tao cannot be equated with God.[23] They are right if we
think of God as an external Creator, a Supreme Being
outside the world, who rules it from a distance. But that
is begging the question. If we admit a totally different
perception of divinity, a perception that proceeds from
within creation, we cannot but recognize that the Tao was
perceived to have *divine* qualities. Chuang Tzu is speaking
of Ultimate Reality when he tries to describe his search:
"If no one else exists, I don't exist. If I didn't exist, I
would not perceive. I am close to the truth, but I do not
know why. There must be some primal force, but I cannot
find any evidence. I believe it acts, but I cannot see it.
I can feel it, but it remains intangible . . ."[24]

The divine transcendence of Tao is also unmistakable
in this attempt at a creed:

Tao possesses reality and substance,
    but no external action or form.
It can be given; not received.
It can be obtained; not seen.
It is its own source and origin.
It existed before heaven and earth;
    yes from all eternity.
It makes spirits and gods divine;
    makes heaven and earth to be born.
It is above the zenith, yet not high;
    below the nadir, yet not low.
Preceding heaven and earth,
    it is not ancient.

Though older than oldest antiquity,
it is not old.[25]

Looking at an old tree we in the West think of God as the carpenter, the architect, the artist who created it and shaped it, from outside. I remember once visiting an outdoor exhibition of sculpture in Arnhem, the Netherlands. One of the artists had placed this notice at the base of a majestic beech: "Statues are hewn by fools like me; only God could make this tree." The Taoists looked at *the inside* of the tree. They saw God present, not as the super-sculptor, but as the primal force from which the tree drew its being and its specific form. Becoming aware of this divine origin was for them "great knowledge", to be distinguished from the "small knowledge" of our petty, every-day existence.[26]

Because of our external approach, we are inclined to see God's presence manifested most clearly in what is marvellous and spectacular. We are moved to think of God when we watch a sunset, a starlit sky, a school of flying fish skimming the waves. We would not normally associate God with ugly things. In fact, we feel embarrassed in our faith because he created what looks evil or imperfect. But the Taoists saw the same divine principle underlie all reality. They meditated with preference on imperfect things: gnarled oaks, hunchbacks, freak pigs with twisted snouts, earthquakes and famine. The Tao is in insects, weeds, mud and excrements.[27]

The greatest difference, perhaps, lies in the Taoist perception of their own involvement. For they knew that the Tao they became aware of in other things was the same Tao living in themselves. That is why the sacred oak could rebuke the carpenter: "Who are you, useless creature that you are, to judge me to be a useless tree?" By getting to know the Tao, one begins to understand

35

oneself. But the opposite is also true. "One only gets to know things by knowing oneself."[28]

Because the Tao is nameless and beyond words; because it lies under the surface of sense perception; because it unites apparent opposites on a deeper level; in short, precisely because it is divine and beyond change and turmoil, it can only be found in silence. This is the greatest paradox and the deepest insight. God is found within, in the apparent void, in the profound emptiness from which all power and life radiates in all directions.

> Thirty spokes share the wheel's hub;
> it is the hole in the centre that makes it work.
> If you shape clay into a vessel,
> it is the emptiness within that defines its use.
> If you cut doors and windows to make a room,
> it is the openings that render it habitable.
> Profit may come from what is there;
> its use comes from the Nothing within.[29]

The Nothing within us is the source of all our energy. It is the well we should more consciously draw from. But how will we, workaholics, activists, busybodies, ever learn to enter that infinite cavity of inner silence and emptiness?

36

4

Horizons Unknown to a Frog in a Well

Taoist teachers, such as Lao Tzu and Chuang Tzu, were practical people. They did not propound a sterile philosophy or academic wisdom. They offered a fuller way of living, a method of surviving the pressures of a chaotic world. Their pupils were professional soldiers, businessmen, tax collectors, magistrates and other civil servants. The secret of success, they taught, lies in knowing who and what we are. Effective action must spring from familiarity with the source of power within us. We will only achieve results if what we do is carried by the Tao.

The Tao flows in us. The Tao is like a river flowing home to the sea.[30] The Tao is like a mighty stream that fills everything. What is so fascinating about it is its way of combining omnipotence and self-effacement. "The ten thousand things depend on it for life yet it makes no pretensions. It does its task yet makes no claim."[31] The Taoists loved the image of water on account of its paradoxical qualities which, for them, expressed what the divine presence, the Tao, is like. "The highest good is like water. Water gives life to the ten thousand things without begrudging them anything. It flows to places others reject. It is so much like Tao."[32]

Sometimes we can be like the Yellow River. In autumn thousands of wild torrents flow into it, so that it swells into a mighty stream. The river laughs, proud of its strength. Boastful and haughty he swings downstream to the coast. There he sees the ocean and his face falls. He tries to measure its vast expanse and fails. He offers his apologies. Rightly so.

Of all the waters in the world
the Ocean is the greatest.
Though all rivers pour into it, day and night,
it never fills up.
Though it returns its water day and night,
it never runs empty.
Its level does not drop in summer.
It does not rise at the time of floods.
No other water can match it.[33']

When we become aware of Tao we realize how all we have is dwarfed by Tao's magnitude. It is a realization that could frighten us and make us feel put down. It should not. Rather, it should reassure us. We too are carried by the same infinite, universal Tao. Knowing this liberates us from our narrow-mindedness. It frees us from our kitchen-and-garden horizon. What is required on our part is the willingness to open up, to embrace cosmic reality. "Can you talk about the ocean to a frog in a well?"[34]

If we want to be close to the Tao in us, we should imitate it. This means we should be like water. Or, to put it in a different way, we should not swim "against the flow". In all circumstances we should study nature and act in harmony with it. The Taoists tell many stories to illustrate this. An old man fell into a river with cataracts and whirlpools. People rushed forward to help him, but did not know what to do: the place was notorious for

38

its fatal accidents. To everyone's surprise the old man clambered ashore after having been under water for a long time. "How did you manage?", they exclaimed. "Easy", he replied. "I knew the stream. I allowed myself to be pulled down by downward currents. Then I came up with an upward current."[35] A cook showed King Wen Hui how to cut up a massive ox with just a gentle swish of his knife. The secret lay in finding the natural lines of the joints, cutting along bones and ligaments, not across them.[36] A wood carver explained to the King of Lu how he had hewn an unusual bellstand out of one trunk. After mental concentration and fasting he spent many days in the forest till his eye fell on a tree that seemed to hold the bellstand naturally in its form. He followed the lines of nature.[37]

The wisdom of "riding on a wave" is obvious. Applications of it can be found in all skills and professions. But we have to dig deeper to appreciate the real point. The old man who fell into the river, the cook and the wood carver acquired their skill because they had come to adopt a new attitude. They had become docile, humble, unassertive; like Tao. In Taoist words they had become like a valley – which adopts an unassumingly low position between ambitious mountain ridges, thus filling itself with life-giving water and flourishing crops. The valley, lying low in silent fertility, is like a woman during intercourse who by her stillness overcomes and fulfils the passion of her partner.

> The spirit of the valley never dies.
> She is the woman, the mysterious mother.[38]

> A great country is the lower reaches of a river –
> the place where the rivers of the world unite,
> the mother of the world.
> Woman overcomes man by stillness,

lying low in stillness.[39]

Why is the ocean king of a hundred
valleys and their streams?
Because it lies in a lower position.
Therefore it is king of these valleys and streams.[40]

The lying low of water is so marvellous because it seems
like non-action, while being highly efficient. The Taoists
called this *wu-wei*, non-doing. It is hard to define this
paradoxical notion accurately. On the one hand it implies
reserve: one does not interfere, is not ambitious, renounces
profit and fulfilment, rejects selfish desires.[41] On the other
hand, one does not neglect one's duties: one looks after
those in one's care, fulfils all one's responsibilities. The
motto is: "Tao rests in non-action, yet nothing is left
undone."[42] It is the way we do it that matters—like walking
without leaving a track; like counting figures without a
bulky score board; like tying a cord without ugly knots.[43]

The strength of water is in its silence. When it is
disturbed, as when a storm whips up high waves on a lake,
water plays along, allowing itself to be temporarily ruffled.
But as soon as the wind subsides, water returns to its natural
calm. It becomes so still and flat that it shines like a polished
mirror.

Still water is like glass.
Look in it and you will see the bristles on your chin.
It is a perfect level
so that carpenters can use it.
If water is so clear, so level,
how much more the human mind?
The heart of a wise person is tranquil.
It is the mirror of heaven and earth
reflecting everything.

Emptiness, stillness, tranquillity,
reserve, silence, non-action:
these mirror heaven and earth.
This is perfect Tao.
Wise people find here their point of rest.[44]

Everything we saw in the previous chapters comes together
in this text. The experience of conscious inner quiet puts
us in touch with the all-pervading silent power of Tao.
Through this silent awareness we reach out and touch God
in us. Whatever we do will now be inspired by the efficient
non-action that characterizes God's own creative energy.
As fish find all they need in water, we find our happiness
and our strength in Tao.[45]

For in spite of its softness and its tendency to lie low,
water can perform amazing feats. It yields. It is supple.
It seeks the easiest way. Yet it does not give in. It achieves
its purpose with indomitable force. This insuperable power
can be ours if we allow Tao to govern our strategy.

Nothing under heaven is softer and weaker than water.
Yet for subduing the hard and the strong, nothing can
surpass it.
The weak overcomes the strong.
The supple overcomes what is stiff.[46]

The softest thing in the world
overcomes the hardest things in the world.
The flimsy substance enters space
that has no room.
That is why I know non-action works.[47]

Water may take time. Eventually it will cut itself a way
through even the hardest rock.
These meditations on water give us an idea of how the

Taoists viewed reality. Let us for one moment return to the scene where the two envoys of the King of Ch'u offered Chuang Tzu the highest post at court. The master, we remember, was standing knee-deep in Pu river. "Leave me alone", he had said. "It is better for a turtle to drag its tail in the mud." We now know all the unspoken things that went through his mind. He looked at the water of the river, admiring its qualities: its life-giving power, its unobtrusiveness, its silence, its strength, its universality and utter simplicity. He knew he was seeing an image of the Tao, the divine Reality that underlies all being; of the Tao in himself.

He had experienced precious moments of contact with that divine Reality. During hours of silent prayer he had felt anxiety and worry ebb away. He had seen the bonds of money, pleasure and position loosen their grip. Even the fear of sickness and death could no longer terrorize him. He had begun to breathe a new freedom, a new joy about the marvel of living. A country needs statesmen and soldiers, it is true; but it would be unwise for him to seek such posts, or be pushed into them by an ambitious monarch. Better to be like water, seeking the lowest place, being a fertile valley where others could find rest and guidance. "Fishes and turtles thrive in water", he must have thought. "I thrive by union with Tao."

5

Faces Modelled
Inside Out

Our scientific knowledge has advanced a lot since the time of the Chinese Masters. We know much more about the size of the universe, the power locked in nuclear structures, the intricate chemistry of living organisms. This does not invalidate the insight of the Taoist mystics; if anything, it makes it more relevant. For science has not, and cannot, answer the fundamental questions of meaning: the origin of being itself, the why and wherefore. The idea of a divine principle, the Tao, underlying all reality makes much more sense, even today, than the mechanist world view governed by dead matter and chance.

Christian mystics have usually seen God as the Other, the merciful God who revealed his infinite love to us, by creating us and saving us. This external approach to God was due to a number of factors: the "otherness" of God in the Jewish and Old Testament scriptures; the architect approach to God in Greek philosophy; the stress on work and achievement in the Western cultures; the focus on sin and human fallibility in Augustinian and Protestant theologies. Western mystics would be inclined to stress the utter dependence and "nothingness" of creatures, and the complete perfection and other-worldliness of God.

43

But there have been exceptions. One of them was Jan van Ruysbroeck, a spiritual writer who lived in Belgium in the fourteenth century (1294–1381). Jan maintained that the proper way to find God is to seek him within us, teaching that the way to God is not the way of philosophy, but the way of contemplation.

Just like Lao Tzu and Chuang Tzu, Ruysbroeck lived in a time of social and political upheaval. The year 1347 brought the outbreak of the "Black Death", the plague which ravaged Europe, killing thirty million people in its wake. That same year also saw the beginning of the Hundred Years War between England and France. From then on hungry armies roamed the countryside, plundering farmsteads as well as cities, reducing most people to poverty and famine. Brabant, Ruysbroeck's native land, experienced a number of severe famines, one of which led to a bloody uprising of the tenant farmers against their landlords. It was a time of suffering and death; but also a time of opportunity for ambitious men. Many a merchant became rich by trading with the right partners. Many a local leader increased his power by joining the winning side.

Ruysbroeck, who had been ordained a priest in 1317, devoted twenty-six years of his life to the apostolate in the city of Brussels. Then, in 1343, he withdrew with two companions to a hermitage in the Forest of Soignes near Groenendaal. It was there, in the seclusion of his small monastery, that he composed most of his eleven spiritual books. But he remained active as a counsellor. Many came to ask for his advice; he travelled from time to time to give retreats and courses.

Ruysbroeck taught that we can only be successful in life if we draw inspiration from God's presence within us. Inner prayer and external action go together: they are the breathing in and the breathing out which together make life possible. "The Spirit of God blows us out so that we

44

can love and perform good acts. Then he draws us in so that we can take rest and find enjoyment in him. This is eternal life: not unlike our breathing the air out of our lungs and breathing in fresh air. What I mean is: we move inwardly in a mystical enjoyment and move outwardly in good works, both in communion with God. Just as we open our eyes, look and close them again, in such a smooth transition that we hardly notice what we are doing, so we die in God and live from God, always remaining united to him."[48]

Our inner union with God, for Ruysbroeck, is an indisputable fact. But how do we become aware of it? Ruysbroeck distinguishes three stages. During the first stage, when we try to live an honest life and seek deeper dimensions, we are drawn to God by brief flashes of insight. "Then the finger of God stirs in our hearts", Ruysbroeck says. He calls this "mediated union", because we are united to God by means of short moments of awareness. If and when we reach a stage of total openness to God, he may lead us into "immediate union", a condition in which somehow we know that God has taken hold of us. It is the glorious night of the second stage. Our mind, though in darkness, is full of light; our will glows with the desire to love God; our imagination is fascinated by God without being distracted by distinct images. Finally, in the third stage, God may, if he so chooses, admit us to "union without distinction", a state of awareness in which we perceive ourselves as lost in God, as basically one with God.

Ruysbroeck does not say that God becomes more united to us as we progress in holiness. God is already united to us. He is united to us all the time; it is only our awareness of this union that increases. For this is precisely the difference between God and the created beings of the world: God is within.

God is more interior to us than we are ourselves. His acting in us is nearer and more inward than our own actions.

God works in us from inside outwards; creatures work on us from the outside.[49]

How are we to understand this inner presence of God? Ruysbroeck explains it by a reference to the scriptural creation stories. Other theologians and mystics had drawn inspiration from the text in which God is compared to a potter fashioning the human person. "The Lord God took some clay from the ground and formed a human person out of it. He breathed life-giving spirit into his nostrils and the man began to live" (Genesis 2:7). It is a beautiful picture. We see God, the supreme artist and craftsman, moulding the clay with his fingers, modelling the human face, shaping the ears, the nose, the eyes and the mouth, and breathing on it to make it alive. A beautiful picture, indeed; but for Ruysbroeck it was incomplete, because another scripture text read: "God created the human person in his own image. In the image of God he created him. Male and female he created them" (Genesis 1:27). The human face, and even more our spiritual personality, did not receive an external mould, but an internal one. The image of God shapes us from within.

To understand Ruysbroeck's point, think of a daughter who looks like her mother. She received the facial expression and other features of her mother, not by some external imprint, but by the genes in her cells. The daughter carries the image of her mother because — as we know now — she has in the nucleus of every cell of her body copies of her mother's chromosomes. This is a modelling from inside. This is, Ruysbroeck tells us, how God models us. "God's image supports the essence and personality of all human beings. Every person possesses it totally and undividedly. And so we are all one, united in our eternal image, which is the image of God; an image which is for all of us the origin of life and existence. Our created being is anchored in that image as in its eternal cause."[50]

If only we knew ourselves, we would know God. For we are the way we are because God makes us so — from within! Our existence as beings who can know and love, the mystery of our individuality, our hunger for meaning and fulfilment, it all finds its source and explanation in God within us.

> According to his or her creatureliness the human person undergoes the imprint of God's eternal image without ceasing; just like an untarnished mirror which always reflects the image and which without ceasing renews our knowedge of our appearance with new clarity. This essential unity of our spirit with God does not exist in itself. It rests in God, and flows from God, and hangs in God, and returns to God as its eternal source.[51]

> The human spirit receives according to its most interior and highest being, in naked nature, the imprint of God's eternal image and God's own radiance without ceasing. The spirit is a perpetual dwelling of God which God inhabits all the time.[52]

Because of our special nature human beings possess this inner presence of God in an outstanding manner. However, the same divine presence, though in a lesser degree, sustains and supports all creatures. For it is God who, from within, gives existence and life and individuality to everything that exists.

> Our essential and highest individuality lies in God. For all creatures exist and live and are preserved by being

united to God. If they were to be separated from God, they would return to nothingness. We possess this divine individuality in ourselves, yet beyond ourselves, as the beginning and support of our existence and our life.[53]

In the highest stage of awareness, Ruysbroeck taught, we are so keenly conscious of the divine presence in us that we lose ourselves in God. We experience what he calls a "union without distinction". We experience, as it were, how God fulfils himself in us. We become God to some extent. Some of his contemporaries accused Ruysbroeck of being a pantheist; that is: of making creatures like ourselves equal to God. But this was far from Ruysbroeck's mind. We are created by God through direct contact from within; we are in no way equal or co-extensive with the infinite mystery of God. "God's transcending nature", he said, "must be understood as oneness and simplicity, unscalable height and unfathomable depth, incomprehensible breadth and infinite length, dark silence and ferocious energy."[54] God himself, though creating us, cannot be touched by the limitations of our earthly existence.

In God is neither time nor place, before nor after, possessing nor desiring, giving nor taking, vices nor virtues, nor visible love, lightness nor heaviness, night nor day, nor anything else that could be put into words.[55]

If Ruysbroeck had known Taoist thought, he would have agreed with its main tenets. Like Lao Tzu and Chuang Tzu he would hold that God is revealed in nature as the underlying divine presence which gives existence, life and shape to all beings. But as a Christian, I am sure, he would have added the dimension of the Tao revealing himself

48

as a Person. I imagine that he would have spoken to the Chinese Masters in these terms:

"You are quite right in saying that the Tao, God, transcends our human imagination to such an extent that human terms cannot strictly be applied to him. We cannot say that God knows, or loves, or wills, or plans, in the way we human beings do. God is the One, as you rightly maintain.

"However, this absolute oneness of God could be misunderstood as if God is vague and indistinct. But the opposite must be true. We know this not only from Christian revelation — which I personally firmly believe in — but also from seeing what God's presence in us does. For if we human beings are made in God's image, God must possess to a superior degree those qualities that we admire most in human beings: our ability to understand, to give love, to communicate and to achieve a purpose we set ourselves. In other words: God must possess *par excellence* the qualities that make up a person. This 'personal' quality of God, however imperfectly we conceive of it in human categories, is surely one of the aspects of the Tao we should acknowledge and respect."

Ruysbroeck would also be in very close agreement with the fundamental attitude of silence and humility demanded by the Taoist masters. He prescribed the same path to his own disciples. Contemporaries described him as unassuming in appearance: quiet and reserved, dressed in simple clothes, walking through the streets of Brussels alone and lost in thought. When invited to address a gathering, he spoke with great simplicity in his native tongue "without any pretension of learning". One biographer contends that his decision to live in the hermitage was triggered by the loud and incessant chatter of one of his fellow priests at the Rectory of St Gudule in Brussels where he was staying at the time! It was the last straw which helped Ruysbroeck to flee the noise of city life and settle in the quiet and solitude of the forest. But what about us today? What can we do to discover the Tao? How can we become aware of God whose imprint we bear all the time? About this we will speak in the next chapter.

6

The Way in
to the Creator

If Lao Tzu and Ruysbroeck were to live in our age they
would offer the following advice. "Love silence", they
would say. "Develop your sense of wonder. See beyond
symbols. Immerse yourself in being. Seek your deepest
Image." And this is what their suggestions mean in simple
terms.

Make sure that you have moments of *silence* every day.
At times these moments may come naturally. At times you
have to create them, to make room for them. Take a stroll
in a park. Sit on the grass in your back garden. Curl up
before a winter's fire. Wherever it is, or during whatever
time of the day, switch off noise both inside and outside
of yourself, as far as you can. Just be quiet and enjoy,
savour, the beauty of silence. It will become your favourite
music.

> Elected Silence, sing to me
> and beat upon my whorlèd ear.
> Pipe me to pastures still and be
> the music that I care to hear.
> Gerard Manley Hopkins

51

In the beginning you may feel uncomfortable. The noise of the day, unresolved feelings, hopes and worries assault you. Do not panic. Just let them ebb away. If you simply practice *tso-wang*, "sitting in silence" (see chapter two), your mind will become still and clear. You will love the sensation. You are preparing yourself for states of deeper awareness.

Having drunk of silence, open your mind to *wonder*. Begin to notice how beautiful created things are; and how complex, how mysterious. Never hurry when you look at things in this way. Take your time while you observe and admire every detail. Think of Chuang Tzu at Pu river studying a turtle. Select something from your own surroundings. Notice its features. Remember, perhaps, new knowledge about it that you have learned in scientific reports. Take it in. Digest it. Allow yourself to be surprised.

After having acquired some practice in thus being "spellbound", turn your attention to people. Watch a particular person. Try to understand him or her. Abstain from making moral judgements but notice what a marvel every human person is; however small or however old. The time will come that you will want to reach out to deeper mysteries.

Become aware of the fact that everything you notice has the quality of being a symbol. You have to learn *to see beyond symbols*. Perhaps you may want to start with trees. Remember the Chinese stories about them (chapter three). Observe a tree's dynamic energy; the strength of its stem, the tenderness of its leaves. See with your mental eye how Tao expresses itself in all those ways. Don't look only at tall, majestic, perfect trees. Observe trees that are gnarled, twisted, bent; with branches lopped off and scars on their bark. Become aware of the same life force irrepressibly popping up in a myriad forms.

Turn your attention to other things; to plants, animals, people. What can you learn from them about the One, about the Ultimate Reality in which they all share? You will feel a longing to belong more closely; to be a conscious part of its overwhelming power, of

—the one interior life
in which all beings live with God,
themselves are God, existing in the mighty whole,
as indistinguishable as the cloudless East
at noon is from the cloudless West,
when all the hemisphere is one cerulean blue.
William Wordsworth

The time for you has then come to plunge even deeper into the secrets of nature. For this you have to let yourself go. Being aware of the unspeakable Reality surrounding you, *immerse yourself in its being.* Think of the image of water, so aptly described by the Chinese masters (chapter four). Admire the flow of the One in all things. Feel how it flows in yourself. Enjoy the thrill. Be happy to be part of it; even when it swirls and eddies mysteriously in ways you had not expected.

Don't say, don't say there is no water.
That fountain is there among its scalloped
green and gray stones.
It is still there and always there
with its quiet song and strange power to spring in us,
up and out through the rock.
Denise Levertov

Understanding the flow in nature, make up your mind to respect it. Decide to act according to the principle of *wu-wei,* "non-doing' (see chapter four). It will give you a mastery of things by not going against the grain. You will not break your body but listen to what it is saying to you. You will not weary yourself doing things at the wrong time in the wrong way. You have discovered the dance of nature and will want to remain in step with its music.

Who sets the tune? Who is the Lord of the Dance? Whoever he or she is, realize you can know the Person from yourself. *You are made in that Person's Image.* Your individuality hangs in that person; flows outwards from that Person (chapter five). The more you probe your deepest self, the more you have an inkling of what he or she must be like. That ultimate Reality, the One, must *at least* be able to know, to love, to communicate, as you can. The only difference, you will realize, is that he or she can do so more overwhelmingly and completely than you.

Recognizing the Person will give new dimensions to your inner experience. Your silence will never be lonely. Your wonder can become a conversation. Seeing beyond symbols you start discerning a Face. Your trust of nature, your harmony with its ways, turns into an act of loving surrender. Your respect for yourself begins to engender a longing for ever closer intimacy with the Person within you.

PART TWO

THE INNER
JUDGE

7

Big Brother's
Watchful Eye

When we were small we probably met God first, or certainly most forcefully, as a Judge. I remember a spiritual reading book we had at home, a picture book designed to teach children religious truths. One picture showed a little boy (me?), precariously standing on a chair in the kitchen, his arms eagerly reaching to the top shelf where Mum had cunningly hidden a box of sweets. Hovering in the clouds high above the kitchen scene was shown the face of God, looking down on the boy (that is: on me) with a frown of displeasure. The caption read: "Mum may never know; God sees everything!" Aware of the punishment that can be unleashed by just an earthly Mum, I was thus warned of the spanking I would one day get from this awesome, inescapable Parent.

We are not a law to ourselves. We have to render an account for the good or evil that we do. A sense of deep responsibility should pervade all our thoughts, words and actions. I firmly endorse these fundamental principles of human morality. What I feel needs to be challenged is the role of capricious tyrant, law enforcer and executioner which has been attributed to God. He is none of these things, as we shall see.

In Christianity we speak of a particular judgement when the individual dies, and of a universal judgement at the end of time when the whole of humankind will be judged. Popular spirituality expressed these truths — often at the expense of other Christian values — in strong images which inspired fear and trembling. Michelangelo's magnificent painting of the Last Judgement in the Sistine Chapel in Rome may be a masterpiece; one only needs to look at the tortured faces of the men and women hurled into the abyss of burning pitch, to capture the dread and terror that lived in the medieval mind. Remember those famous stanzas of the *Dies Irae* hymn which describe the last day so graphically:

> Day of wrath! O day of mourning!
> See fulfilled the prophets' warning!
> Heaven and earth in ashes burning!

> Oh, what fear man's bosom rends
> when from heaven the Judge descends,
> on whose sentence all depends!

> Wondrous sound the trumpet flings.
> Through earth's sepulchres it rings.
> All before the throne it brings!

> Death is struck, and nature quaking —
> all creation is awaking,
> to its Judge an answer making.

> Lo! the book exactly worded,
> wherein all has been recorded;
> thence shall judgement be awarded.

> When the Judge his seat attains,

and each hidden deed arraigns,
nothing unavenged remains.

What shall I, frail man, be pleading,
who for me be interceding,
when the just are mercy needing?

King of majesty tremendous,
who dost free salvation send us,
fount of pity, then befriend us!

Righteous Judge of retribution, ·
grant thy gift of absolution,
ere that reckoning-day conclusion. . . .[56]

Before discussing what is wrong in this picture from a Christian point of view, I would like to turn to Islam, where the idea of God's judgement has been worked out in even greater detail. We have all the more reason for doing so because there have been some great Islamic spiritual masters who replaced the traditional view with a more profound, mystical understanding. But first, let us see what Islam teaches about God as the Judge.

The Koran which contains the revelation given through Muhammad, describes Allah, God, as compassionate and merciful, but also as the king of the day of judgement (Sura 1,1). He is the wisest of judges (S. 95,8), who rewards the good (S. 9,120–1), but whose wrath destroys the wicked (S. 7,97–9). He is swift in taking account (S. 24, 39). He tests all (S. 3,142, 154) and sees all (S. 3,163). His decrees are unalterable (S. 6,34; 18,27). No one can escape his judgement (S. 27,83–90).

The scene of Judgement Day is described in 39 of the 114 chapters of the Koran. The Jewish/Christian image of the judgement is reinforced. People will be judge

59

only on their good or evil conduct, but also on their acceptance or rejection of Allah's revelation:

> We have sent you a message from our presence. Whoever turns away from that message, truly shall carry a burden on the day of judgement. Grievous on the day of judgement shall it be for them to bear.
>
> That day shall come with a blast on the trumpet and we will gather the sinners on that day bleary-eyed (with terror). . .
>
> Humble shall be all faces before Allah — the Living, the Self-Subsisting, eternal; forlorn shall be the person who carries the burden of iniquity, but whoever shall have acted rightly and who has believed shall fear neither wrong nor loss of reward.
>
> That is why we sent down to you an Arabic Koran explaining therein instruction in detail, so that people may fear Allah. . .[57]

In order to face God with tranquillity on that last, terrifying day, religious people will naturally want to know what precisely God demands of them. Organized religion obliges them by enumerating precise prescriptions. In Islam we find, first of all, the five "pillars": the confession of Allah as Only God; prayer five times a day according to precise formulas; fasting during the month of Ramadan; almsgiving; and making the pilgrimage to Mecca if at all possible. These principal requirements were soon augmented by numerous smaller prescriptions contained in the *Shari'ah*, a code of laws based on verses of the Koran and oral traditions. Typical rulings of the Shari'ah are: the circumcision of males, the prohibition of wine and pork, principles of marriage and divorce, the laws of inheritance.

It is obvious that principles and norms are helpful to guide people and groups of people in their conduct. What is characteristic of much *religious law* is that it claims to express in precise detail the actual will of God. In a recent document, "The Universal Islamic Declaration", this concept is expressed again:

There are no intermediaries between Allah and man. Allah's guidance is available to all in the form of his Book al-Qu'ran and in the life example of his prophet, the Sunnah (tradition). . . The Shari'ah is the supreme law of the Muslim community and must be enforced in its entirety in all aspects of life. Each and every Muslim country must explicitly make Shari'ah the criterion by which to judge the public and private conduct of all, rulers and ruled alike, and the chief source of all legislation in the country. . . Obedience to the legitimately constituted authority is obligatory on people only as long as it is in conformity with the Shari'ah . . . Islam exhorts the believers to strive incessantly to establish Allah's will on earth.[58]

The Shari'ah *is* the will of God! And, if we question its logic or appropriateness, we are referred back to Allah's absolute authority. The very irrationality of many of the requirements, we are told, is a test of the believer's devotion.[59]

Now it is precisely this aspect of God as lawgiver and judge which, in my view, needs to be challenged. Since God is our creator, as we believe, what could be his motive in revealing special laws? Does it not show up a defect in his original creation? What could the function of such laws be? To put the problem in perspective, I would like to present it as a parable, one which I request sensitive readers not to take as a mockery of religion. Our purpose is to get to the root of a very important spiritual absurdity.

61

Once upon a time there was a headmaster who ran the only school in his home town. In order to get jobs and to advance in life, all children had to attend this school. The headmaster only allowed children to enter the school on certain strict conditions.

Little boys were only admitted if they had their right ear lobes cut off in the rite of "concision". Girls were allowed to attend class like the boys except for geography; this was a subject totally forbidden to them. Three times a day the bell was rung. Then all teachers and pupils were to rise from their seats, turn in the direction of the headmaster's office and bow deeply. The little sweet shop outside the gates and the canteen in the school offered sweets and refreshments; but under no circumstances was any student to eat chocolate or drink Pepsi Cola. Questions about the reason for such rules were met with a curt demand for blind obedience.

On assessment day the headmaster would call all children together in the assembly hall. Large registers were opened in which the actions of each pupil, good or bad, had been meticulously recorded. Those who had done well were given a pass. Those, however, who had failed in any way, and particularly if they had sinned against the special rules, were humiliated in public. They left the school with empty hands, doomed to carry the burden of their evil deeds.

If the story seems crude, why is it so? If God acted as such a headmaster, would he not inspire more fear than love? And what about the treatment of the pupils? If God were to treat us in like manner, would it not show a lack of regard for the autonomous judgement with which he endowed us at creation? How could we justify the revelation of divine laws that seem capricious and irrational? Could

God's will really be like the petty capers of a narrowminded headmaster?

Throughout history people have claimed to know "God's will". To fulfil "God's will", Christians and Muslims slaughtered each other during the Crusades. "God's will" was invoked to start wars, conquer more land, persecute heretics and witches, deprive people of their freedom. Some Christian Boers in South Africa justify apartheid as "willed by God". In fact, religious fanatics at all times have covered deeds of violence and unspeakable atrocities with the excuse that it was "God's will". The more absolute the revelation adhered to, the stronger was their conviction and the more extreme the injustices they inflicted.

But the question of "What is God's will?" arises equally in smaller matters. Consider, for instance, the question of clean and unclean food. A Muslim, we are told, may not eat the flesh of any animal which is forbidden by Allah. This includes: wild animals, birds of prey, pigs, animals that creep. However, birds with long flattened beaks (except crows) are permitted to be eaten. Birds with hooked beaks (except parrots) are forbidden. Hare and rabbit are permitted. The drinking of wine or the milk of a mare is forbidden (though this does not include the milk of a she-donkey). Most important of all, the flesh of an animal may only be eaten if the man slaughtering the animal utters the words "Bismillah, Allahu Akbar" ("In the name of Allah, Allah is the greatest"), otherwise it may not be bought or eaten. The flesh of animals slaughtered with the help of machines is strictly forbidden.

These, we are told, are the rules of *halal*, which is defined in this way: "*Halal* means the eating of those things only which have been permitted by Allah. One who does so will be rewarded by Allah; and one who does not do so will be punished by Allah."[60] The implications of such rules are quite clear. Orthodox Muslims in Europe, for instance, cannot eat meat served in any ordinary restaurant, for the food will either include forbidden meats, or the "bismillah" formula will not have been used!

If some external action is considered to be "God's will", the temptation will be great to define the requirement of that action to the last, and often the most ridiculous, detail. This is what happened in the Catholic Church through the so-called Sunday Mass obligation, until the reform of Vatican Two. The ancient Christian custom of celebrating the Eucharist on Sundays had become an "ecclesiastical law" by the time of the Middle Ages. In the nineteenth century moralists hammered out the finer points of this obligation, the transgression of which, they asserted, was a mortal sin (which means: deserving eternal punishment if not repented and forgiven!). To fulfil the obligation, they decreed, one should attend at least the three principal actions of offertory, consecration and communion. These three parts, however, could be added up from different services; so that if one arrived halfway through one service and attended a communion, it was enough to take part in the offertory and consecration of a further service. It was, they said, fulfilling the external obligation that mattered. Even if one was mentally distracted throughout the service, one had fulfilled the obligation. Or if the person had been in church on a Sunday for some other reason (to do some repair, or as a tourist) and afterwards realized that it was a Sunday, he or she had still fulfilled the obligation by being physically present when the Eucharist took place.[61] This is what an excessive stress on the external action can lead to. The clever moral theologians knew precisely "what God willed"! But did they?

8

Layer upon
Layer of Radiance

It is tempting, especially for members of so called revealed religions, to consider conformity to external law as the highest proof of moral goodness. Muslims, for instance, might think that observing the "five pillars" and the rules of the Shari'ah make them true Muslims. Since God's will is identified with the laws, keeping them means being in harmony with God. On the day of judgement all God needs to do is to check our external behaviour against his list of prescriptions!

This way of looking on things is obviously wrong. One of the great theologians who pointed this out was Abu Hamid Muhammad Al-Ghazali (A.D. 1058–1111). For simplicity's sake I will call him Ghazali. His influence both inside and outside of Islam has been extensive: European scholars have called him the greatest Muslim after Muhammad; Muslim writers have given him the titles *Hujjat al-Islam* (which means "proof of Islam") and *Muhyi id-Din* ("reviver of religion").

Born in Tus in Iran and educated in Jorjan and Nishapur, he quickly gained the reputation of being a great scholar. In spite of his youth he composed learned treatises which are still classics in Muslim theology: "The Inconsistency of Philosophers", "Revival of Religious Sciences" and "The Golden Mean in Belief". In the year 1091 the Vizier Nizam al-Mulk appointed him chief professor of the Nizamiyah College in Baghdad. Only thirty-three years old, he now occupied a top position in the Muslim academic world.

By all accounts it looked as if Ghazali's career was made. Then one fine October day, four years later, came the crash. . . More than three hundred students had crowded into his lecture room, a record for the time. Prayers had been said. The audience had taken their seats. The shuffling of feet and hubbub of voices subsided. All eyes were fastened on the young and famous lecturer. Ghazali consulted his notes. He opened his mouth to speak, but not a sound came. . . Drops of sweat stood on his forehead. . . Suddenly he picked up his notes and walked out of the lecture room. Later, in an autobiographical account, he described the moment. "One day I had prepared myself to give a lecture to satisfy the desires of my students. But my tongue refused to utter a single word. I could not do a thing. . ."[62]

His breakdown was due to a deep inner conflict. Ghazali knew that from a human point of view he had made it. By using his mental skills in teaching and by conforming to conventional religion, he could strengthen his position all the time. With it wealth, social prestige and even political power would come his way. At the same time he realized that this is not the way God needs to be served. God looks at the heart. God was appalled, he felt, at his externalism and his unworthy motives. If he was to be true to the dictates of his own heart, he would need to give up his glorious career and seek God in a life of poverty and detachment. It was the life-or-death choice between conformity and real sanctity. "I deliberated on this for months, the options before me all the time. One day I would resolve to quit Baghdad; the next day I would

66

abandon my resolution. I put one foot forward and drew the other back. In the morning I would feel a genuine longing to seek eternal life; by the evening a multiplicity of other desires would have reduced it to impotence."

The final outcome was Ghazali's breakdown. He left Baghdad and retired to solitude for eleven years. Only towards the end of his life did he take up lecturing again, this time in Nishapur. By then he had regained enough inner security to be able to undertake such an external responsibility without danger to his integrity.

Sufis like Ghazali believe that God is interested first and foremost in people's hearts; not in their external behaviour as such. Though opinions may differ on what constitutes the essence of Sufi practice and belief, there can be no doubt about its universal search for deeper realities. The Sufi tries to dig deeper than organized religion; he studies hidden meanings, and commits himself to transcending truth. The difficulty in understanding what Sufis teach is often precisely their reluctance to express their fullest beliefs in words. Their deeper intuitions and understandings are only expressed to the closed circle of initiated students.[63] Sufis walk to God on the path of direct perception and religious experience. "The heart of the believer is between two of the fingers of the Merciful", Ghazali would say.

I believe that Ghazali has expressed his approach to God best in a small mystical treatise entitled *Mishkat al-Anwar*, "The Niche for Lamps".[64] The fifty-seven pages of the Arabic manuscript are not easy to decipher. Ghazali employs the academic language of his day, and writes in terse formulations. He says more than once that he does not wish to write more clearly, so as not to offend those who might not understand. It was only by carefully reading his tract again and again, and by putting together information dispersed through various chapters, that I could obtain a rather complete grasp of his teaching. To present it meaningfully to contemporary readers requires a good deal of "padding out" and dynamic translation. If Ghazali could speak to us today, he might, perhaps, talk to us in the following manner.

"Many people imagine Allah is far away. They believe we cannot see him because he reigns high in heaven as creator and judge. There are even atheists who claim Allah does not exist; simply because they do not observe him in nature or in their every-day surroundings. However, to a person with insight Allah is very close indeed. Such a person becomes aware of Allah's immediate presence in everything that exists.

"We can see things with our ordinary, physical eyes because of light. Actually, we do not see those things themselves, but we see the light that comes from the sun and that is reflected from those things. In fact, although the light is so common and obvious, and although it is really only the light that we see, we may be under the impression that light cannot be seen. The very intensity of light's presence is the direct cause of its apparent invisibility.

"Now the same applies to our seeing on a deeper level. Everything that exists exists because of the light of being that comes from Allah. This light of existence we may call 'Allah's face', or 'the aspect of Allah'.[65] Since everything owes its being to Allah, in all things that do exist nothing exists except Allah and his face.[66] When we look at things on the level of reality and being, we are actually seeing 'aspects of Allah', 'the face of Allah'.

"'But I'm not seeing Allah', you may object. Remember what happens to physical seeing and light: we do not see light precisely because it is the means of seeing everything. In the same way, the reason why we fail to see Allah's face is because it is so intensely present and all-pervasive.

68

Materialists will not rise to this kind of vision, of course. Philosophers will argue to Allah's reality from the 'signs' they observe in creation. But people with a true spiritual insight become aware of Allah's overwhelming closeness. Their spiritual eyes are opened and they suddenly perceive that all existence is exclusively Allah's face. Nothing has substance or individuality that does not come from Allah.[67]

"Just as everything is manifest to our ordinary eyes by means of light, so everything is manifest to our spiritual insight by means of Allah; for Allah is with everything every moment and by Allah does everything appear. And, just as in the case of ordinary light which is invisible on account of its intensity, so Allah's obscureness to those who cannot see his presence results from his very obviousness. His elusiveness is due to the very radiance of his brightness. With some justification we can say that Allah hides himself from his own creation by his utter manifestness! Animals in the forest cannot see him, though human beings can.[68]

"This ability to see Allah in everything is due to the extraordinary human privilege of having a 'spirit' or 'soul'. For this is like a spiritual eye. Without physical eyes sunlight could not be seen. In the same way, human beings would not be able to perceive Allah on a deeper level without the inner mind. It is because of this inner mind that a human person can be said to have been created after Allah's image.[69] Since human intelligence judges everything according to the principle of truth, it is infallible when left to itself.[70] The mind is Allah's balance scale on earth.[71] Reflecting Allah's inner light it has a part that is absolutely clear and self-luminous.[72]

"We could also put it in this way. The presence of Allah is engraved on the tablet of the human heart. A man's or woman's inner self carries the form, the image of Allah. It is as if Allah expressed himself in it; or, inversely, as

69

if everything in the world is summed up in the human image, an image which Allah inscribed in his own handwriting. Thus we can say that a human person is the divine handwriting. This leads us to a very important conclusion. Whereas one can see Allah present in everything, as I have explained before, we can see Allah even more clearly in ourselves. We may truly say that only that person who knows himself or herself knows Allah.[73]

"'But doesn't that mean that we ourselves are Allah to some extent?!', you might say. Yes, it does. Some mystics have been deeply aware of this unity between themselves and ultimate reality. They have uttered statements that would seem incomprehensible to simple believers, such as: 'I am the Real!' 'Glory be to Me. How great is My glory!' 'I am He whom I love and He whom I love is I; we are two spirits dwelling in the same body.' Such visionaries, however, must not be taken in a very literal sense. They were so overwhelmed by seeing Allah *in* themselves that they could not express this better than by saying they felt like *being* Allah.'"[74]

So far Ghazali's reconstructed little sermon: does it make sense? I think it does if we keep a few things in mind. Seeing God's face in everything that exists may seem a tall claim. But, suppose for a moment "being" and God are synonymous. Suppose everything has God in as far as it "is". Then everything that has being manifests God to us, to the extent that it is. It opens a whole new way of thinking. It gives us especially a new attitude towards ourselves; because instead of looking on God as the one who stands opposite us, we suddenly recognize him as the one who manifests himself in our own being!

Now Ghazali, being the great theologian he is, does not make the mistake of literally considering being to be identical with God. What he tells us is that "being" is

God's *face*. In everything that exists, God manifests something about himself because he is the one who gives it being and who supports it in being. In our own personality too, whatever we *are* tells us something about God. Having been made in God's image, we human beings, more than other creatures, express in ourselves something about God. The more we know ourselves, the more we know about God.

This presence of God in everything was sought and sung by Sufis of all times. Ibn al-Arabi (1165–1240) expressed it daringly by the statement that "the existence of created things is nothing but the very essence of the existence of the creator".[75] God's existence flows, as it were, like the sea under its waves, through the fleeting forms of individual beings. God can therefore be seen in all the facets of our life: in what is drab or exciting; in what is normal or extraordinary; in everything that draws our attention. An ancient Sufi recital puts it in these words:

A light flickers in the grey of dusk — you are there.
A pagan performs a dreary ritual — you are there.
A reflex movement — you are there.
Not only in what the scribe writes, but in his smile
    —you are there.
In the charm of a beautiful lady, if not in her mind
    — you are there.
A question and answer: if not in them then
    in their interplay — you are there.
The elephant takes his lumbering paces — you are there.
Whenever there is agreement
    or love
    or being
    or truth
    or finality — you are there.
The oyster-fan rejects a pearl — you are there.

In things chaotic,
   out of tune
   in transition — you are there.
In touch, heartbeat, delight, silence, rest:
in whatever fits and does not fit — you are there.
In the glow, the spark, the fiery flame, the heat and
the burning; in what relaxes and excites—
   you are there![76]

In making these observations Ghazali comes to a position similar to that of the ancient Taoist Masters and some Christian mystics. He too sees God the creator *inside* creatures rather than as their external cause. But Ghazali goes a step further, which will help us in our present discussion. For it is also God, as lawgiver and judge, who shines forth from our heart. The human mind, which is God's balance scale on earth and the infallible assessor of truth, becomes a new, inner principle of morality, directly opposed to externalism and slavish conformity. We will see more about this in the next chapter.

Ghazali's book, "The Niche for Lamps", is based on a beautiful verse, the so-called Light Verse in the Koran (S. 24, 35), a text that has inspired Sufis throughout the centuries. We are like an oil lamp with God the flame within us. His light radiates from the centre outwards, transfusing the oil, shining through the glass container and illuminating the niche.

Allah is the light of heaven and earth. His light may be compared to a niche holding a lamp: the lamp is encased in glass, the glass shines like a twinkling star. Its sacred oil. . . is luminous though the fire itself does not touch it. Thus we see his radiance in layer upon layer.

72

9

The Ant, the Stone
and the Pitchdark Night

One of my teachers in primary school loved a poster
that displayed a large eye within a triangle. "This is
God looking at you", she would tell us. "He sees
everything!" It was a standard warning to deter us from
the various kinds of mischief we engaged in while she
turned her back. "You cannot escape God! He is your
judge and he is watching you all the time!"

Muslims too believe in this all-seeing Judge. The Koran
tells us: "He observes everything. No eyes see him; he
sees all eyes" (S. 6,102–3). "He knows all things. . . He
observes all your actions. . . He sees the very secrets
of the bosom!" (S. 57,3–6).

But if God's sight is so keen that he even sees the
leg of a black ant on a black stone in the thick of night,
as an Arab proverb has it, what precisely is he looking
at? "Whether your deeds conform to the law",
traditional Muslims might answer. "No!", the Sufi
replies. "Whether your heart is full of love!" The God
of conventional religion measures performance by the
scale of the law; the God of the heart judges a person
by his or her conscience.

To see the practical implications of this consider the function of the K'abah. It is a small shrine located in the centre of the great mosque of Mecca. Muslims consider it the most sacred spot on earth. It is at the K'abah that the pilgrimage ends with a walk seven times around the shrine. It is towards the same K'abah that Muslims have to turn for their prayers five times a day. In every mosque a niche called the *qibla* indicates the direction of the K'abah. A sacred tradition records an assurance by Muhammad that a prayer offered in the holy K'abah earns a reward equal to a hundred thousand prayers elsewhere.

The importance traditionalists attach to the direction of the K'abah annoys the Sufi temper. Do we turn towards the K'abah because God is there?, they would ask themselves. Their answer was: "No! God is not out there, far away in Mecca. He is right in our heart!" Jalal ad-Din Rumi (A.D. 1207–3) wrote a beautiful poem about it.

I examined the whole of Christendom and the cross.
He was not on the cross.
I entered the Hindu temple, the ancient pagoda.
He was not to be seen.
I ascended the highland of Herat and Kandahar.
My search was in vain.
He was neither on the heights nor in the valleys.
I climbed the peak of Mount Kaj.
Nothing I found but the nest of the Anqa bird.
I visited the K'aba of Mecca.
He was not there.
I asked Avicenna, the philosopher, about him.
He was beyond Avicenna's reach. . .
Finally I looked into my own heart.
It was there, in his own place, that I saw him.
He was nowhere else.[77]

God is not in the K'abah, but in the heart! Innermost consciousness and loving heart can find God in the most unlikely places, Ibn al-Arabi, would say: in the tablets of the Torah or the leaves of the Koran; in the pilgrim's K'abah, but also in the temple of idol worshippers, the church of Christian monks and a meadow feeding gazelles.[78] Other Sufis said simply: "Consider the curve of your eyebrow as the edge of your prayer niche. There is no real difference between the K'abah and a pagan temple — wherever you may look, God is equally everywhere!"[79]

This is quite revolutionary talk if we remember the rigid obedience to external practice expected in traditional Islam. In fact, one prominent Sufi, Al-Hallaj (A.D. 858–922) was condemned to death because of a remark he had made about the K'abah. It may be that he had attracted most hostility because of his mystical claim to be in union with God ("I am the Real!"); but the official ground for putting him to death was Al-Hallaj's assertion: "More important than going on a pilgrimage is to proceed seven times around the K'abah of one's heart".[80] The prosecution also adduced a letter written by Al-Hallaj in which he had advised a believer that instead of going to Mecca, one could draw a square in the central part of one's house and perform the same rites around it as one would have done in Mecca.[81] Al-Hallaj died a terrible death. He was scourged, one hand and one foot were cut off, he was nailed to a gibbet; and then beheaded after six hours.

Small wonder that later Sufis were more careful in what they said or wrote in public. To retain their inner freedom, they often had to hide their true beliefs from the suspicious scrutiny of traditionalists. At times they would maintain conventional teaching for outsiders, while giving a different interpretation to their close disciples. Those "on the level of the Shari'ah" cannot understand deeper things.[82] But the bloodhounds of external law had smelt blood.

The Qur'anic Law had only legislated for an external tribunal and punished public sins. . . The canonists and professional theologians, very displeased at seeing people speak of searching their consciences and judging one another by this inner tribunal, tried to show that the ultimate results of the life led by mystics were heterodox. For the mystics held that the intention is more important than the act, that practical example is better than strict letter of the law and that obedience (in spirit) is better than observance.[83]

Did the Sufis reject external law? They did not. Law was helpful, they maintained, because it contained guidance. But it was not in itself the *absolute* will of God. It had a symbolic function. It pointed to a deeper, inner reality. Men and women would, in the last analysis, be judged not by external conformity, but by obedience to the dictates of their consciences. Let us listen again to an explanation by Al-Ghazali.

We put off our sandals when entering a mosque; or before kneeling down on our prayer mat. Moses was told to put off his sandals in the presence of Allah (Koran 20,12). Pilgrims approaching Mecca put off their sandals at a certain point. What is the meaning of all this? Is Allah really bothered about us wearing sandals or not? Is he upset when we wear them at prayer?

When we put off our two sandals we make a symbolical gesture. We indicate detachment from the two worlds: from the world of earthly pleasure and the world of spiritual reward. We indicate by this gesture that we want to serve Allah alone, for his own sake. Now do not think on that account that the external action is useless. Precisely because it has this inner meaning, we should be faithful to it. We should combine

76

fidelity to symbolic ritual with the intention of the heart. When Moses was told by Allah "Take off your shoes", he understood that Allah meant: "Renounce the two worlds". He obeyed the command literally by putting off his two sandals and spiritually by detaching himself from the two worlds. This is the spirit in which we should observe external prescriptions![84]

As to turning towards the K'abah when we pray, the same thing applies. Of course, we should follow this practice if we can. But we should not for a minute think that we do this because Allah is more present in Mecca than elsewhere. The Koran says clearly: "In whatever direction they turn themselves there is the face of God" (S. 2,115). In fact, the name of God, *Allah*, is derived from the root *wly* which means "turning". He is the one towards whom all faces are turned — by which I mean especially the faces of the hearts of men and women for they are truly lights and spirits.[85]

The mind, Ghazali tells us, is aided by philosophies. "Now the greatest of philosophies is the word of Allah in general and the Koran in particular. Therefore the verses of the Koran, in relation to our mind, have the value of sunlight in relation to eyesight."[86] Elsewhere he tells us that percipient spirit (whether the eye or the mind) "is as important as perceptible light; no, it is more important because it is the percipient spirit which apprehends and through which apprehension takes place".[87] Therefore the human mind, which "breaks through into the inwardness of things and into their secrets"; which "covers the entirety of existence passing upon them judgements that are both certain and true"; which left to itself "cannot err because it sees things as they are"; which is "created after Allah's likeness and the sample must be commensurate with the original", and which may be called "Allah's balance scale on earth" is the ultimate norm by which a person will be judged.[88]

This principle of conscience made many Sufis accept that the highest religiousness transcends organized religions. Jalal ad-Din Rumi could say: "What can I do, Muslims? I do not know myself. I'm not a Christian, neither a Jew, nor a pagan, nor a Muslim!"[89] An Indian Urdu song exclaims: "Muslim, Hindu, Christian, Jew and Sikh — brothers in a secret sense; yet who knows it in his heart?. . . All is He, my friend, all is He!"[90] Ghazali himself in one of his other books deals explicitly with the question of salvation for non-Muslims. Only those who willingly and knowingly refuse to accept revelation will be punished, he asserts. God's mercy will embrace all who follow their honest conviction. "I would say that the majority of Turks and Byzantine Christians of our time come under the divine mercy, God willing."[91]

For Sufis, what matters is finding "the pearl". This pearl is the discovery that God is everywhere; especially in our hearts. It is this discovery and true inner conversion that make a person holy, not religious observances. It is not the multiplication of practices or the proximity to holy things that count in the end. "A thread does not become a jewel by passing through the holes of a series of pearls."[92] "A donkey stabled in a library does not become literate."[93] In the conflict between observance and inner devotion to God, inner devotion should prevail.

A Sufi disciple once said to his master: "I'm surprised that anyone who believes in God should not attend the mosque for worship." The master's reply was typical. "I am surprised that anyone who has a personal experience of God can pray to him without losing his senses and thus render his ritual prayer invalid."[94]

I would like to conclude this chapter with a Sufi parable

describing the life journey of an individual. God is present in the cloud, the ocean, the shell and — the pearl!

A drop of rain fell from a cloud. Looking down at the ocean it said: "Who am I compared to this vast expanse of water?"

A clam, touched by the raindrop's humility, opened its shell and received the drop inside; which turned into a pearl.

10

The Mirror and
the Lens Inside Us

Islam and Christianity are two major world religions that claim to have received a direct revelation from God. Both believe in a universal judgement when God will reward the good and punish the evil. In both religions there has been a tendency towards externalism as if God, an external judge, bases his verdict on external transgression or observance. We saw that within Islam Sufism rebelled against this trend.

There are many Christians, too, who by sheer ignorance have become ritualists and practitioners. However, the basic message of Christianity is unmistakable. It agrees in substance with the Sufi position. God looks at the heart. He has given every individual a conscience; and it is according to this conscience that people will be judged. Whereas in the Old Testament there still was an external code of law, Jesus Christ abolished that system of law and replaced it with inner grace. The law of the New Testament is the Holy Spirit speaking in our hearts. We carry in us not only the voice of God which tells us what to do and what to avoid; we also carry God's love, which urges us to do the right thing.

Documenting this central Christian doctrine exhaustively would go far beyond the space available to me. I will briefly explain the Roman Catholic belief, which is very much representative of what most other Christian Churches hold. I would like to start with conscience itself. Psychologists have tried to derive its origin from a "super ego". Anthropologists have said it is partly inborn, partly learned from the clan and society in general. Christians will generally feel that these explanations, though containing elements of truth, do not adequately explain the whole phenomenon of conscience.

John Henry Newman (1801–90) has written some wonderful pages on conscience. With the awakening of human reason all men and women have a sense of right and wrong. This is truly an amazing fact. For, if we analyse the dictates of our conscience, we observe that they are based not on personal advantage, or pleasure, or the expectations of society, but on some objective norms. We know, for instance, that murder is wrong, that helping a person in need and seeking the truth are praiseworthy. These are not mere animal instincts; they show our inner awareness of a moral law that is part of the universe to which we belong.

Our consciences, Newman points out, evoke feelings of either guilt, reproof and disgust, or peace, joy and praise. Because they are *feelings* they show involvement with a Person. "Conscience is always emotional. This means that it involves the recognition of a living object towards which it is directed. Lifeless things cannot stir our affections. Affections respond to persons. . . Moreover, the kind of feelings we have prove that the feelings of our conscience are directed to a person who is supernatural and divine. We feel good or guilty even if no other human being knows about it. This proves that we have within us the image

81

of One who is good and who expects us to live according to the reason he gave us."[95]

In a story about early Christianity Newman makes a pagan child speak about her conscience. It is a moving description which sums up accurately the experience of people in all religions.

I feel God within my heart.
I feel myself in his presence.
He says to me: Do this. Don't do that.
You may tell me that this command is
   a mere law of my nature,
    as it is to rejoice or to weep.
I cannot agree to this.
No.
It is the echo of a person speaking to me.
Nothing shall persuade me that it does not
ultimately proceed from a person external to me.
It carries with it its proof of its divine origin.
My nature feels towards it as towards a person.
When I obey it, I feel satisfaction;
when I disobey, a soreness just like that which
I feel in pleasing or offending some revered
   friend.
Believing in God I believe in what is more
   than a mere "something".
I believe in what is more real to me than sun,
moon, stars, the earth and the voice of friends.
You will say, who is he?
Has he ever told you anything about himself?
No, he hasn't.
But I will not give up my conviction.
An echo implies a voice; a voice a Speaker.
That Speaker I love and fear.[96]

In his letter to the Romans Paul has stated clearly that the natural law is written on people's hearts, and that everyone will be judged according to his or her conscience (Romans 2:14–16). This makes Christianity radically an interior religion. The Catholic Church has endorsed this recently in the pronouncements of the Second Vatican Council (1963–65). "Conscience is the most secret core and sanctuary of a person. There he or she is alone with God, whose voice echoes in his or her depths. In a wonderful way conscience reveals that law which is fulfilled in the love of God and the love of one's neighbour."[97] It is on account of this principle that the Church proclaimed its declaration of inner religious freedom for all. "People are bound to follow their conscience faithfully in all their activities so that they may come to God, who is their final destiny. Therefore no one may be forced to act contrary to his or her conscience. Nor may any person be prevented from acting according to his or her conscience, especially in religious matters."[98]

But if conscience deals with natural law — the law infused by creation — what about the laws revealed by Christ? Do Christ's words in the gospels, and the prescriptions laid down by the Church through the centuries, not constitute a new law which Christians have to obey as God's will for them? The Christian answer is: No! As Paul explained so clearly in his letters to the Romans and Galatians, Christ abolished all law. As Christians we live directly under God's grace. By living in our hearts in a new and marvellous way, God gives us the inner love and strength to live up to the requirements of our vocation.[99]

In simple terms, this is what Christians believe: in natural religions — and the Old Testament was still part of this — people's relationship to God is perceived as taking place through intermediate structures. To obtain favours one performs rituals and sacrifices. One has to observe feast

83

days, customs and taboos. One relates to God through sacred places, sacred persons and sacred objects. This whole network of external structures is a "system" standing between the human person and God. Laws are part of this "system". Jesus, however, destroyed this kind of "system" and established a direct relationship with God. Each person is linked immediately to God, who lives in his or her heart. Whatever structures remain — such as sacraments, ministries, church laws, and so on — have only a subsidiary function. They support; they are not important in themselves.

Thomas Aquinas (1224–74), for instance, who is rightly considered by many to be a paragon of traditional orthodoxy, attributes to external laws only a secondary role. "The new law of Christ", he tells us, "consists mainly in the grace itself of the Holy Spirit which is inscribed in the hearts of the faithful. The written law comes in the second place, and then only because it offers helps which dispose people to receive grace or give guidance as to how to use that grace." He goes on to explain this in the following terms:

Everything should be understood according to its principal element. However, the principal element in the law of the New Testament, the thing that constitutes its total quality, is the grace of the Holy Spirit which is given us by faith in Christ. Therefore the new law is mainly the grace itself of the Holy Spirit. This is clear from what the Apostle Paul states when he says. . . : "The law of the Spirit of life in Christ Jesus has set me free from the law of sin and death" (Romans 8:2). Therefore also Augustine stated that "as the law of the Ten Commandments was written on stone tablets, so the law of faith has been written on the hearts of the faithful". And elsewhere he says: "Which are those laws of God which he has written in our hearts, if not the presence of the Holy Spirit himself?" There are, however, some guidelines which the new law contains, which dispose people to receive the grace of the Holy Spirit or which help the correct use of that grace. These occupy a secondary place in the new law. Also about these guidelines the Christian faithful should be instructed in words and writings, both regarding things to be believed and things to be done. Therefore I conclude once more that the new law is mainly the inner law, only secondarily a written law.[100]

The law of the Spirit is, in a manner of speaking, the Holy Spirit himself. "The law of the Spirit is identified either with the person of the Holy Spirit or with the activity of that same Spirit in us." "The Holy Spirit himself is the New Testament in as much as he works in us the love that is the fullness of the law."[101] That is why we can say that the new law justifies us; that it forgives sins and makes us holy. This is another reason why it is different from any written law.

Thomas works out the implications:

In the Old Testament a law was given externally so that sinners were struck with fear; here, in the new dispensation, the law is given within so that sinners can be made holy. . . That is why the Apostle Paul says: "The letter kills, but the Spirit gives life" (2 Corinthians 3:6). And Augustine points out that here with "the letter" is meant every written text existing outside people, even the text of moral precepts such as are contained in the Gospel. That is why even the letter of the Gospel would kill unless there would also be present inside the grace of faith that heals.[102]

The new law for Christians is the Holy Spirit who fills the heart with love and enables it to respond. Written laws play a supporting role. They give suggestions, hints, directions; as a guide leading us to Christ (Galatians 3:24), or as traffic signals marking out the straight and narrow road (Matthew 7:13–14). They challenge those who have lost the way. That is why Paul can say: "The law is not made for the just, but for the unjust" (1 Timothy 1:9). The external laws, though helpful, can never replace the inner law of grace and love.

Putting these thoughts together we can draw some important conclusions. When God created us he gave us human reason which functions as our conscience. He wrote on our hearts principles of truth and justice that go beyond our own narrow self-interest. It is according to the dictates of our conscience that we will be judged. When God revealed himself in Jesus Christ, he did not impose an external law but filled our heart with the Spirit of love. Again it is on our response to this inner Spirit that we shall be judged. Does it not follow from all this that we carry inside us the God who will judge us?

To say that we are responsible only to ourselves would be ridiculous; for right and wrong are values that transcend us. It would be as ridiculous as believing that we created ourselves. But to say that our highest judge is God *in us* makes sense; as it makes sense to say that the Creator manifests himself most clearly in us. If I can know God the more I know my true self, I will be faithful to God the more I obey my deepest sense of right and wrong. To know the divine will I must, in the final analysis, turn inwards and listen to his voice.

In *Hamlet* Polonius, chief counsellor of Denmark's King Claudius, concludes his advice to his son Laertes with a famous admonition:

To thine own self be true,
and it must follow, as the night the day,
thou canst not then be false to any man.

The formulation restricts the norm to loyalty between human persons. But the adage could be extended in a theological sense. "To thine own self be true, and it will follow like the night the day, *to God* thou canst not then be false." For being true to ourself, we will heed the stirring of our conscience and the prompting of the Spirit. Being true to ourselves we are then being true to God who is our inner judge.

This way of looking at things frees us from the mistaken idea that God is pitted against us; that he is our adversary, our task-master from whose anger we want to escape. It saves us from falling into the trap of external practice and ritualism. It stops us from judging other people too rashly; forgetting that they too carry the inner judge. Above all, it gives us a new sense of self-respect and dignity. It makes us treasure the resonances of God we feel in our heart.

The light of God is reflected in our deepest self. All great mystics use the image of the mirror in us: Chuang Tzu, the Upanishads, Ruysbroeck. . . Ghazali reflects on it in a beautiful passage.

I see a patch of light on the floor
of my room.
I look up. It comes from the moon.
It shines through my window, strikes a
mirror on the wall and reflects from it
down onto the floor.
Again I look up, at the moon.
Suddenly I realize that the light of the moon
is itself reflected from the sun. . .[103]

There is light in my heart. There is light in teachers and guides. There is light in external laws. The ultimate source of all this light is God.

Or again we may think of our inner self as a lamp. God is shining from within. Our human individuality, searching for truth and reaching out to wholeness, focuses that light. The sharper the lens, the clearer his image will be. But how can we learn to discern the light? How shall we make contact with its Source? The next chapter offers some suggestions.

11

The Way
in to the Judge

Confronted with our present-day world Ghazali, Thomas
Aquinas and other spiritual teachers might tell us: "Stand
above unworthy desires. Commit yourself always to face
the truth. Refine your sense of good and evil. Remain open
to guidance. Cherish the light in your deepest Self." In
plain language these suggestions might be translated as
follows.

Make sure that you do not become the slave of petty
likes and dislikes. *Keep yourself free from unworthy desires.* How
will you be able to govern your life if you can't say "No"
to yourself? If you regularly eat too much? If you drink,
smoke, watch TV or do other things you know to be harmful
beyond a certain limit? There is nothing wrong in enjoying
such things at the proper time, in the proper place and
within their proper purpose. There is much wrong with
you if you cannot stop; if there are petty attachments that
rule your conduct. Are you moody, lazy, spiteful or jealous?

Since wholesomeness of spirit and body is your ideal,
decide to remain free. Exercise some self-discipline. Go
without things for a while rather than allow them to chain
you.

Our capacity for discontent
let me observe
is in proportion to our desires;
that is in proportion to the intensity
of our attachments
to things of this world.

Thomas Mann

As much as silence is needed to create space for awareness, so a healthy detachment provides a climate in which sensitivity can grow. You will love yourself more, feel healthier and have time for happier pursuits.

Reflect on *the value of truth* in your life. Observe that truth is truth whether you like it or not. Something remains true, the opposite false, even if you lie about it or try to deceive yourself. Admire this amazing permanence of truth. Notice that it acquires this property from its identity with "being". Remember Ghazali's insight in the matter: the quality of "reality", "being", "truth" in everything is Allah's face. Wherever you look, recognize that face.

If you continue to reflect on the nature of truth, your most remarkable discovery will be that your inner self cannot but admit the truth of truth. You carry God's face within you. Be happy about this. Rejoice about the fact that you *are* committed to the truth. Make up your mind to support this commitment fully. Want to unmask the subtle strategies by which we at times have learnt to escape from facing the truth. Decide to be truthful when speaking to others, unless diplomacy is called for in exceptional circumstances. Your love of the truth prepares you for greater sensitivity.

Every person has in himself or herself *a sense of right and wrong.* Have you ever consciously examined this gift in yourself? Have you probed the depth of your conscience? Why is it that you know so clearly that cruelty, theft and murder are wrong; kindness, justice and honesty right? Is it not part of your nature to distinguish moral good from moral evil?

> Cowardice asks, Is it safe?
> Expediency, Will it bring me profit?
> Vanity asks, Is it popular?
> But conscience, Is it right?
> William Morley Punshon

If you study your conscience when it is at work, you will notice that it rests on two pillars: your feelings and your reason. Through your feelings you naturally empathize with other people. If carefully listened to, your feelings sharpen your sense of what is human, what is not. But the final umpire, the referee who really decides, is your mind. Your power of reasoning is "Allah's balance scale in your heart". Listen to your feelings but most of all to your common sense. Together they cannot fail.

Of course, you are not alone on earth. Others have faced the same problems you have, and it would be very shortsighted not to avail yourself of their experience and wisdom. Therefore, adopt an attitude of *openness to guidance*. This guidance may be contained in parental advice; in traditions and customs; in religious practices; in rules and regulations. Some of these rules are so important for society that they are enforced by public sanctions. Realize that there is a good reason for this in most cases. Allow yourself to be guided; though remembering all the time that your own judgement has the last word. Ultimately you are responsible yourself for what you decide to do.

Considering your ultimate responsibility will inevitably lead you *to confront the mystery of your deepest Self*. Light radiates from within you. Will you capture its rays, reflect them respectfully and focus their brilliance on your daily life?

Or will you choose to be "a child of darkness"? The more you become sensitive to the light, the more you discover it has a face. It shows itself to you at times as the Truth; then as the Absolute Good; then as the Ground for humanity and justice. Your power to assess, to judge and decide derives from God, who is the final judge of all.

Then, with D.H. Lawrence, we may

> feel the presence of the living God
> like a great reassurance,
> a deep calm in the heart,
> a presence
> as of a master sitting at the board
> in his own and greater being,
> in the house of life.

PART THREE

RESCUING GOD FROM OUR THINKING

12

Sparks from the Mind's Furnace

I am sure that at this stage some readers may feel as did a friend of mine, with whom I was discussing the inner approach to God. "I'm aghast", she said, "to hear such nonsense. We know what God is like. The Bible tells us so. Philosophers have proved his existence, his nature, his qualities. Why throw overboard what the best of minds have worked out in centuries?"

I was speechless because I realized that, from her point of view, the matter was closed. How to tackle her rather simplistic ideas? How to explain in a few sentences the complicated history of human thinking about God? How to convince her of the obvious truth that our ideas about God are of our making and thus inaccurate? "Then on the shore of the wide world I stand alone and think", I told her; but I knew I was doing her an injustice. What she needed was the opportunity to study religious history; and to think about thinking itself. This is what we will do in this section.

Most people imagine thinking to be a very straightforward action, just like sleeping and walking. Thinking seems so simple and natural. But in fact, few people stop to examine their mode of thought; they take their thoughts for granted. Yet many problems in life take their origin from our thoughts. As we read in Hamlet:

> There is nothing either good or bad
> but thinking makes it so.

So far in this book I have challenged wrong concepts about God, and especially the unwarranted stress on his action outside us. The time has now come to place my contentions within the wider frame of human thinking about God. If we study the history of that thinking we can see more clearly why a certain bias was unavoidable; that is, until now.

Of necessity the chapters in this section will be a little more academic (and thus boring?) than those in previous sections. Some readers may find philosophy stuffy, abstract arguments contrived, and ancient heart-searching out of date, so for their sakes I will try to strike a balance. I will attempt to keep my text lighthearted — though whether I can succeed in this when wading through the morass of medieval metaphysics, I do not know! But for more serious students who, like myself, believe that even mental muddles can be fascinating, I will provide solid and extended notes, notes which will, in fact, offer a substantial *reading guide* to all questions I touch upon.

Experience over hundreds of years has shown that it is useless to speak of God before we start examining our way of thinking. This is not an excuse or an escape, but a real necessity. If theology means reflection on God, it is by definition bound up with thought. Whatever meaningful word be uttered about God is ultimately based on a category of our mind. It is too much to say that God is "the product of human minds", as Julian Huxley maintained, but it *is* correct to say that our *understanding* of God is the product of our mind. Just as music cannot

96

be played without an instrument producing the notes, so our speaking of God rests on the quality of our thinking.

Thinking can be of different kinds, much as there are different approaches in the sphere of action. Originally men and women travelled on foot. Later they trained the horse and covered greater distances on horse-back. Later again they mechanized transport, and even took to travelling by air. Walking, riding on horse-back and flying in an aeroplane are three totally different approaches to the same action of travelling. They are three *kinds* of travelling, related to the same basic need of going to another place, but meeting this need with different techniques.

To cut stone people first invented the hammer and the chisel. Then they invented dynamite. Later still they found the chemical solution for making cement, thus enabling themselves to make concrete of any kind and shape required. The basic purpose of using stone for construction is still there, but radically different approaches of doing so have been developed. The same is true of human thinking.

In the course of centuries we have developed some fundamentally different approaches in our thinking. These ways of thinking are just as different from one another as walking is different from flying. We have developed the new ways of thinking out of necessity, as we have developed better techniques of cutting stone in the struggle for survival.

It will now be my purpose to show the three main kinds of thinking which humankind has developed, and to explain how they are different. The three kinds I refer to are called: mythopoic, metaphysical and functional.[104] **Mythopoic thinking** is the kind of thinking that sees coherence in the world by the presumed existence of invisible, supernatural agents in our immediate environment. **Metaphysical thinking** understands reality as a universal, all-embracing whole, subject to the same laws of being.

97

Functional thinking limits the understanding of the world to particular aspects of it, and those only in as far as they are seen to have a meaningful function. As these definitions are too abstract to permit a concrete grasp, I will work out the difference by means of examples.

Mythopoic thinking

Recall the way in which an orthodox Hindu approaches the mystery of "fire". For him fire is a manifestation of the god Agni. In ancient times people used to make fire by rubbing two pieces of wood together, and whenever the spark as "a living being" sprang out of that dry wood, this was considered a supernatural event, a creative act of Agni. The aggressive nature of the fire god was derived from the fact that as soon as it was born it began, with unnatural cruelty, to consume the parent wood from which it had sprung. Agni is a god who brings prosperity, but also a god who makes heavy demands. In the Mahabharata it is recounted how Krishna sacrificed a whole forest, with all living beings in it, to the hunger of the god Agni. The "homa" is the Hindu's sacrifice of fire in which ghee and other precious materials are offered to the god.

The supernatural nature of fire is attested to in everyday Hindu religious superstitions. If a person dreams that his house is destroyed by fire, it is reckoned to be a very auspicious sign. The fire of a lamp will never be placed towards the south, the abode of death. Fire may not be lent out at night to another person. One should never wear a burnt cloth. Most of all, the function of fire is sacred at the cremation of the dead body. It is a handing over of one's body to the god of fire. In ancient days the wives of a deceased husband would voluntarily throw themselves into the arms of fire.

This wood and sacred oil, O Lord of fire,
I offer hoping it will enhance your power.
As best I can I worship you with hallowed words.
I seek a hundred blessings through this hymn.

Grant us your favours, generous Lord,
rich as you are when brightly enkindled.
With your shining arms and flickering shapes
bring your treasure to my home.[105]

If we analyse this kind of thinking we find it rests on the assumption that under the appearance of fire there is the supernatural agency of the fire god. It is the fire god who is supposed to bring prosperity and protection. It is also the fire god who ultimately claims life. The reality of every-day fire is linked with the imagined action, the "myth" of the fire god. That is why this kind of thinking is called "mythopoic", that is "myth-making".

Metaphysical thinking

The Greek philosophers approached fire in a totally different way. They asked themselves fundamental questions about the universe in which we live. Looking at the reality around them, they were convinced that it was ruled by some basic laws that would apply to everything. Aristotle in particular stressed that underlying the many different external forms of beings, there is a homogeneous construction of the world. In this fire too has a part to play. Heraclitus even maintained fire was *the* basic constituent of the universe.

Following Empedocles, Aristotle maintained that all substances in this world were a combination of four elements, namely: fire, air, earth and water. These four elements were distinguished on a logical basis. Warmth and coldness, dryness and wetness are the primordial qualities, Aristotle said. The four elements are distinguished because fire is warm and dry; air warm and wet; the earth cold and dry; and water cold and wet. The elements also differ in their tendencies of upward or downward motion. Earth and water are "heavy" and tend downwards, while fire and air tend upwards. That is why, according to Aristotle, the elements in their pure forms lie on one another in layers: the earth underneath, then the water, then the air and finally fire.

Lucretius, like other "atomists", disagreed with these views. The smallest units of matter, he claimed, are "atoms": tiny, solid particles, permanent, indivisible, capable of being the building blocks of any known object. Atoms are more basic than fire.

> Those who thought that the raw material of matter is fire have obviously strayed far from the truth. Also those who say there are four elements. . . In visible objects there is a final point that forms the smallest thing that can be seen. Similarly, there must be a final point in objects that lie below the limit of sense perception. This point is indivisible and the smallest thing that can exist. . . If there were no such indivisible atoms, even the smallest bodies would consist of an infinite number of parts, since they could always be halved and their halves again halved without limit. . . But this cannot be. Reason cries out against it![106]

Notice that Empedocles, Aristotle and Lucretius tried to go beyond observing physical reality. They arrived at their conclusions by argument, by logical thinking. They practised what Aristotle called *metaphysics*, that is: what comes after and goes beyond physics. Metaphysical thinking tries to understand the nature of things. It argues by general laws. It approaches reality by considering over-all qualities that can be applied to reality as such.

Functional thinking

In modern thinking fire is approached once more in a different way. If we strike a match, we see a flame leap up from the stick. The scientist asks: "What happens?" His answer will bear upon the chemical reaction. At specified degrees of heat, material substances tend to combine with oxygen. This is a rather violent reaction which changes the original compound drastically (by, for instance, reducing wood to ashes) and releases energy in the form of heat and light.

This understanding of fire may seem simple and straightforward to us now, but it took scientists centuries to establish the chemistry of combustion. Until late in the eighteenth century scientists generally followed George Ernst Stahl, who proposed the phlogiston theory. In fire, he said, a substance which he named "phlogiston" escapes from the burning fuel into the air. "If you invert a drinking glass over a burning candle, the flame dies out because it is stifled by the phlogiston with which the air within the glass is saturated." In spite of his scientific intentions, Stahl still adhered to the Greek notion that fire — now under the name "phlogiston" — is an element of matter.

Antoine-Laurent Lavoisier discovered the true nature of combustion in 1772, by careful measurements. On weighing the remnants of burned sulphur, he found these ashes were heavier than the original substance. This could only come about by the chemical combination of the original sulphur with an element in air, namely oxygen. A flame under an inverted glass dies out because the oxygen in the air gets depleted.

To arrive at such important new insights scientists had

to overcome both mythopoic and metaphysical thinking. The modern scientist is not interested in the "nature" of fire in a philosophical sense, but in how it can be used in technological processes. After having analysed the components of fire, the scientist studies its applications. On the strength of his studies he designs furnaces to cast iron or blow glass. He makes engines with which the combustion of fuel can be converted into energy. Most of our modern machinery, from the steam engine to the Jumbo Jet, derive their energy from carefully controlled processes of fire. The scientist knows how fire works, and he makes it work for us.

When studying a phenomenon such as fire, a scientist will limit himself to what he observes and what he can deduce with certainty. He only claims to have *functional* knowledge. He would feel it to be wrong for his conclusions about fire to be applied to other fields of experience, unless they be proved. He will not admit *a priori*s and generalizations.

†

Primitive people ascribe a fire to a supernatural agent, the metaphysician tries to understand its being, and the modern scientist tries to find out how it works. Each of these three modes of thinking springs from a different phase in the development of humankind, and is still part of our mental framework. Each has deeply affected our understanding of God. For God too can be approached from various angles and can be thought about in varying terms. The difference does not lie in fire or in God, but in our mental make-up. Our mind is, after all, the apparatus with which we think that we think, as Ambrose Bierce reminds us in his *Devil's Dictionary*.

Have you ever looked into a flame and reflected on

its mystery? Have you seen a forest go up in fire and shuddered at its destructive power? Have you been spellbound by the wild beauty of glowing coal in an open hearth? You will then have no difficulty in entering into the world of mythopoic thinking, a world we are now about to enter.

> I praise you, God, divine fire,
> my priest,
> minister of my sacrifice,
> who offers my oblation,
> who gives me all I treasure.[107]

13

The Power Perception of Ancient Myths

Mythopoic thinking developed in the earliest ages of human existence. It probably arose as soon as the human mind was able to consider the world with some degree of abstraction. It may have begun more than a hundred thousand years ago, when small clans of human beings roamed from one hunting place to another in East Africa, Southern Europe or the sea coasts of Asia. Mythopoic thinking was our ancestors' first attempt at understanding reality.

Let us put ourselves back into humankind's situation at the time. Relying on archaeological evidence and adding a little from our imagination, we may reconstruct people's day-to-day life in quite accurate terms. Let us imagine enjoying the rare privilege of meeting a typical tribal group on the coast of the Mediterranean about 100,000 B.C.

We find the human family sunning itself and playing on the beach in an ideal spot. A little river flows near by — so necessary for supplying drinking water, for they have not yet invented pots and jars. There are some rocks with overhanging cliffs under which they can find shelter — they do not yet have the ability to construct artificial houses. And the edge of the evergreen forest remains within walking distance — that is where they have to hunt for their daily meat.[108]

When we approach the group we may find them in a relaxed mood. They have just finished eating a reindeer, cut to pieces with chips of stone and distributed raw. Zalu who is sitting in the centre is their undisputed leader. He is naked, brown and hairy. He makes the impression of being a wary and tough person. Baka, Talin and Teka are other adult men, Zalu's brothers. The rest of the group are women and children of various ages. The whole clan is one big family, with Zalu as the patriarch.

At first sight this human family would look to us very much like a troop of chimpanzees or gorillas. Many of their habits and customs seem so much the same. But soon we notice important differences. These human beings walk erect. Their hands are better equipped for precise work. Their eyes look more intelligent. And, above all, they can speak, even though their words are simple and short. If we watch them during the hunt or when preparing food we observe other features which we would never find with animals. Before undertaking any work they *plan* their action together. And to achieve their purpose they use instruments: pieces of wood, stones, animal bones or whatever seems to fit the need.[109]

An interview with Zalu would prove an enlightening experience. Presuming that he was prepared to speak to us (after lengthy introductions, and with the help of an interpreter), he might describe his hunting expedition in words such as these:

"Zalu belly ache. Men belly ache. Children belly ache." (He means: *Yesterday everyone felt hungry*). "Men dance. Men power-catch reindeer." (*Yesterday evening the men performed a religious dance during which they killed a symbolic reindeer that had been drawn in the sand.*) "Moon power-fill night. Moon power-fill men." (*Because of the moonlight the men felt confident they would make a good catch.*) "Men enter forest, walk, walk. Men see reindeer, power-circle reindeer, run, catch reindeer. Zalu kill reindeer."

Analysing Zalu's speech we would find a limited number of categories. His thinking is bound up with the immediate, visible realities of his world: the forest, the men, the moon, the reindeer. Most of his thoughts move in the realm of hunting, food, family, travel. His thinking has the main task of expressing and organizing his external behaviour: his walking, running, throwing, cutting. Zalu does not distinguish clearly between things, animals and persons. Of course, he knows that there is a difference, but this difference is not fully grasped. For him all things are alive. The sand, the river, the tree, the moon, the reindeer are living realities he has to face.

A little reflection will show that we need not be surprised at this. *We* know that water flows because by gravitational laws it seeks the lowest place. Zalu thinks water *walks* as he walks. For him the sun, the moon and the stars are mysterious living beings influencing his life. When Zalu tries to understand this world, he will see in all things around him manifestations of "life" or "power". Moonlight is "power". Rain is "power". Plants, trees, animals and children grow by "power". Accepting such a mysterious "power" is an intellectual necessity for Zalu, for it is the only thing that makes sense of his world. Believing there is such "power", he need not be surprised at the inexplicable events of his daily life: the ebb and flood of the ocean, storm and lightning, an earthquake, the birth of a baby in the womb of his wife. This is the origin of Zalu's religion.[110]

The birth of myths

Studies of anthropology and comparative religion prove that people slowly developed the idea of a divine reality, "power", as distinct from the profane reality of everyday life. The concept of "tabu", of the sacred prohibition, is one of the oldest religious notions of humankind, a notion derived from it. According to this notion one should avoid certain places, things, animals, practices or words because they would bring a person into conflict with the underlying divine "power". The concept of the "sacred" also grew out of this mode of thinking. This means that certain places (hill tops), days (new moon), things (stones), animals (the bull) and so on were considered to be especially filled with the divine reality. People would naturally tend to seek "power" from living contact with these sacred realities. After some time the divine "power" experienced in such sacred objects and events was concretized in the form of "spirits" or "gods". This was no doubt how the idea of "God" arose.

When our ancestors conceived of the notion of "power" as a way of understanding reality, they produced the first "myths". Anthropology defines myth as the display of a structured, predominantly culture-specific, semantic system which enables the members of a culture area to understand each other and to cope with the unknown. In other words, myth is the way in which some important notions of a particular culture are related to one another. Myths are often expressed through stories in which the so-called "strong components" of semantic systems (systems of understanding the world) are symbolically represented.[111]

To explain this, let us return to Zalu. Zalu will always hunt in the same way. He will first draw a reindeer in the sand, dance around it, and then beat his stick on the figure. He will hunt at night, preferably during the full moon. He will never kill pigs, for they are tabu. In this way he may follow many particular customs which are important to him. Asked about a reason for observing them, he might tell the following myth (here freely translated into our twentieth-century way of speaking):

"Once upon a time Rabu-Rabu our ancestor walked through the forest and saw a heavy sow, pregnant and ready to give birth to many young piglets. Rabu-Rabu saw that she was full of power, but he laughed to himself. He knew he should have respected the motherhood of the sow, but in his pride he did not care. He cornered the sow and clubbed it to death. He gave it and its young to his wives and children as food. But Rabu-Rabu's dearest wife and eldest son died. And when Rabu-Rabu went into the forest again, he could not catch any animal. For many days he roamed around, hunting in vain. His wives and children cried for hunger. Rabu-Rabu was desperate. And in the middle of the night, while there was a full moon he wept. And the moon took pity. She came down to Rabu-Rabu and showed him how to draw a reindeer on the sand, how to dance round it and how to power-catch it. Rabu-Rabu learned this art and caught a reindeer during that very night."

This kind of myth, of which we have many examples in primitive cultures, superficially resembles a simple story. We might be inclined to ask: Has it happened or not? But this would be a sorry misunderstanding. To Zalu the story does not express something of the past. It explains relationships with which he is vitally concerned in the present. It unifies the "strong elements" of his world, such as hunting, reindeer, pig, moonlight, and fixes a norm by which he can judge them. For him the truth of the myth lies in the validity of the "structure" which he imposes on the various "strong elements" of his experience.[112]

As people's thinking grew more conscious and myths

108

more explicit, the notion of good and evil spirits, or gods and goddesses, became more pronounced. Often such "gods" as those related in the myth, were nothing more than personalized expressions of a power which had been experienced. Zalu would speak of the moon as a "goddess", because that expressed to him the fact that he was successful in hunting on moonlit nights. But calling the moon a goddess necessarily entailed a mental picture or image of her. And having an image of her, he embellished it with a face, with weapons or with characteristic actions, until the moon goddess slowly became a real personality to him — never actually seen, but always thought to be present and encountered in her manifestations. So the idea of "God" and her existence was born from the myths of primitive society.[113]

Archaeology and comparative religion tell us that the most ancient representations of God which have been found are small statues of the mother goddess or the goddess of fertility. It shows that people felt the need of symbolically expressing to themselves the reality of the God shaped in their mythopoic thinking. The idol shaped in their hands was a copy of the notion that had earlier been shaped by their thoughts.[114]

Pitfalls in myths

Primitive people "made their gods" because they needed gods to understand the world. The historical origin of most religions can be traced to this beginning. And mythopoic thinking is not restricted to primitive humankind alone. We may safely say that many religious convictions rest on the same grounds as those found with our ancestors. Even today many people believe in divine powers, and pray to them, because they are overcome by the same basic fears and lack of understanding that characterized our early ancestors.

It does not take long to realize that such a mythological basis for religious convictions reveals many inherent weaknesses. First of all, it looks as if the existence of God itself derived not from actual fact but from the inner psychological necessity of primitive people. Many modern scientists, and especially psychologists, have maintained that belief in God is no more than an escape from a feeling of inadequacy in day-to-day living. As a young and weak child needs a father to support and protect him, so primitive man and woman needed the father figure of God to give him or her the psychological feeling of protection. Although the rejection of all belief in God on this ground is not justified, as I will explain presently, we have to agree that a purely mythological basis for accepting God will not do. Just as exaggerated reliance on one's parents makes it impossible for a person to be mature and independent, so a believer may never tolerate that his or her so-called dependence on God be a psychological substitute, that makes up for his or her lack of maturity.[115]

Another obvious defect of the mythological approach lies in its inability to discover the real nature of God. Because mythopoic people see the divine in every sphere of nature, they are likely to experience God under the most diverse forms. The history of natural religions confirms this fact. Mythological thinking leads to thousands of different kinds of god, usually representing different powers of nature: the gods of the sun, the moon and the stars: the goddesses of beauty, prosperity, fertility and wealth; the gods of storm, rain, lightning, of health and many other things. In many religions, external objects and animals have been considered as direct manifestations of such gods. In this way even the most unlikely animals, such as cows, monkeys and snakes, have come to be worshipped as divine.

The reason for this development is clear. In mythopoic thinking logical argument has no place. It is not kept in check by a critical mind. It does not distinguish between God himself and what God brings about. It does not have the power of reasoning, by which contradictions between various statements can be pointed out and corrected. The confusion of polytheism is the immediate result of mythopoic thinking.

Mythopoic thinking necessarily considers God in human terms. This gives rise to another basic defect of its approach, namely its tendency to attribute anthropomorphisms to God. In primitive people's thoughts, God eats, drinks, walks, sleeps, fights very much like a human person, even though he will do so in a very special way. All the Hindu gods, for example, marry or get married, as if they are sexual beings. They are imagined to have hands, arms, legs, a stomach, and all other parts of the human body, even if these differ from human organs in size and number.

Anthropomorphisms continue to exist in all major religions. Even though Muslims and Christians reject anthropomorphisms on principle, in actual fact many of them still think of God in anthropomorphic terms. They imagine God sitting on his throne high in heaven, listening to the prayers of human beings which come up to him from all over the world. A Christian may say: "God hears my prayer", as if God possesses ears! Or he may say: "If you do this God will be angry with you", as if God has moods like any human being! If we examine our own thinking about and speaking of God, we may discover that it is full of anthropomorphic expressions. To some extent this is unavoidable, as I will show later, but at least we should be aware of the imperfections inherent in this type of religious thinking. If God is God, he simply cannot be small like us. Our imagination plays tricks on us.[116]

111

The value of images

Wherever real human reason began to flourish, it started to tackle the weaknesses of mythopoic thinking. We will discuss this more fully when dealing with metaphysical thought. For our purpose here let it suffice to note that mythopoic thinking, when left to itself, has all the inborn defects of emotional judgements. A teacher at school may like one of her pupils at first sight. But she should realize that such a spontaneous attraction is not the same as an objective, impartial judgement. The mythological approach to God springs from people's emotional reaction to reality: it proves an ambivalent road to walk on.

Considering all the inadequacies of the mythological approach, we might be tempted to reject it altogether; but this would be a mistake. It is true that we cannot rely on a piece of poetry when we need evidence in a court case. Yet a poem does contain something valuable. It often expresses a gem of truth not found elsewhere. Shelley once said: "Poetry is the record of the best and happiest moments of the happiest and best minds." Poetry expresses the intuition or insight a person has of reality at a particular moment.

> What hast thou, Man, that thou dar'st call
>   thine own?
> What is there in thee, Man, that can be known? —
> Dark fluxion, all unfixable by thought,
> Vain sister of the norm — life, death, soul,
>   clod —
> Ignore thyself, and strive to know thy God!
>   Samuel Taylor Coleridge (1772–1834)

Just as poetry catches an aspect of reality through intuition, an aspect which it expresses emotionally, so in mythological

112

thinking an aspect of reality is grasped through intuition and expressed with feeling rather than with cold reason. It thrives on images rather than words.

Intuition is a valid way of grasping reality. S. Radhakrishnan describes it in this way:

> When a region of blurred facts becomes suddenly lit up, illuminated as it were, to what do we owe this enlightenment? It is due not so much to a patient collection of facts as to a sudden discovery of new meaning in facts that are already well-known.[117]

He also calls it a "synthetic insight", "which advances by leaps"; a "deeper consciousness"; "an intuitive experience". This is the kind of experience primitive people had when they "understood" that the world around them simply could not be explained without a "super-worldly power" that made it what it is.[118]

Mythopoic thinking led to polytheism, anthropomorphism and idol worship. Yet it gave people the first intuitive grasp of the religious aspect of all reality. With their slowly awakening intellectual powers, men and women could see what animals had never seen: the presence of the divine. They saw the glimmer of that light, and groping for it they blundered into many blind alleys. But it was a true light and should be recognized as such. Human knowledge made equally sure but limping progress in other areas of life. If properly corrected by rational thought, mythopoic intuition is a good starting point in our search for God.

In ancient Indian thought we find good examples of the way in which mythological thinking can give rise to valid religious meditation. Consider the notion of the divine as the "athma", the "breath" of all existence. This immanence of the divine, this discovery of God's presence in the very

113

substance of created things, flows spontaneously from the mythological perception of "divine power". If suitably corrected, as in the following text, it opens our eyes to a valid aspect of reality.

He who dwells in the fire,
yet is different from the fire,
whom the fire does not know,
whose reality shows up through the fire,
who controls the fire from within. . .
He is your Self (Athma),
   the inner controller, the immortal.
         Bruhad Aranyaka Upanishad III,7.

Many modern authors, following the example of Rudolf Otto, make the fact of religious experience itself the starting point of their apology for God. All people and all nations give testimony of some spontaneous respect for the "holy", for what is "numinous", "divine", "supernatural". Even if in many cases this experience is linked to irrational fear of the powers of nature, the experience itself remains valid. Civilized and educated people also have this experience.[119] In fact, the deep religious insights of the Taoist Masters sprang from this experience.

Before we draw up the balance sheet, let us see what critical thinking said about God. . .

14

Deep but
Dry-as-dust Deductions

To understand the further development in human thinking about God we have to remember the profound social changes that have made us what we are now. From hunters and nomads we have become city dwellers.

About 10,000 B.C. a revolution took place in the history of humankind: our ancestors discovered the possibilities of agriculture and changed over to a settled existence. This change-over seems to have taken place in more than one continent at roughly the same period. The first permanent settlements were established precisely where we would expect them, viz. in the low lands bordering on large rivers. The valleys of the Indus, the Ganges, the Euphrates and the Nile provided the fertile, easily irrigated river banks which enabled families to stay in the same place and live.

People had been engaged in some agriculture for tens of thousands of years before, mainly in the form of reaping natural crops. The new development consisted in the fact that they now learnt the art of sowing the seed and so procuring the crop themselves. This kind of agriculture soon proved a more reliable means of securing food than hunting. It also enabled larger groups to stay together.

115

But switching over from hunting to agriculture as the principal source of food procurement entailed some other drastic changes.

Human families now had to stay in one place. They had to build permanent shelters, and so they invented huts and houses. They also needed new and better tools, which led to the development of skills and crafts. There was the need for storing things from harvest to harvest, and the need for keeping things in the home. The first vessels were made of straw, then of straw covered with clay. Then people discovered the art of baking earthenware pottery from mixtures of clay and finely cut straw. Someone invented the wheel and the axle. Women devised new ways of weaving cloth from agricultural products. In sites of the most ancient cities such as Jericho we can follow the rapid transformation from hunters to craftsmen with amazing precision.[120]

One important consequence of the new life style was the social structure it produced, viz. the "polis", the township. The accumulation of wealth in the homes of the new agricultural community made it a ready prey for thieves and robbers. People had to organize themselves against such attacks from within and without. This they did by electing a leader who would fight for them against their enemies. The leader soon acquired definite rights. Exact boundaries of land were demarcated. The homes of the community were surrounded by a protecting wall. The rights and duties of all citizens had to be laid down. In this way the small kingdom, the township, arose.

By this new way of life people acquired one great advantage: stability and continuity. Human thinking was led into a new direction. Instead of being exclusively concerned with the day-to-day struggle for survival, people could now devote themselves to an exploration of all their talents. The birth of civilization brought about the first

116

flourishing of all the arts: of music, with the invention of scales and instruments; of painting, with increasingly daring artistic creations; of sculpture and architecture; of writing and literature. People invented the sports and the games, the celebrations and rituals with which they could fill their newly found time of leisure. Because of the stability of their existence people could now spend time on the building up of wealth and culture.

In their old existence as hunter-gatherers, people had undergone life in a somewhat passive way: it was as if things happened to them rather than that they took an active part. But now it was different. They began to *organize* their own life, to order, to plan, to fit things together and to construct. They learned by experience the two processes of construction: the break-down of material into manageable components, and their re-assembly into new structures. People's *thought* followed the same pattern: analysis and synthesis; abstraction and re-integration in logical frameworks.

Solomon was a typical city builder. The Bible mentions the new sciences which Solomon fostered. "He spoke of plants, from the (huge) cedar that grows on Mount Lebanon to the grass that sprouts from the wall; he spoke also of beasts, and of birds, and of reptiles, and of fish" (1 Kings 4:33). Notice how in these "listing" sciences two logical processes are involved: distinguishing by categories objects such as plants, beasts, etc. (abstraction); and arranging them in a logical order (e.g. from the biggest to the smallest plant).

From a more superficial abstraction of general properties people could not fail to arrive at a consideration of the most fundamental properties, such as beauty, goodness and being. From cataloguing material objects they necessarily came to the quest for an interlocking view of all reality. People learnt to ask questions, to argue, to reject what

117

was wrong and to accept logical deductions. It is in the town civilizations of the Indus Valley[121] and of Greece[122] that this real philosophical speculation was born.

Proving God by reason

Primitive tribal people had had the intuitive insight that reality was filled with a divine presence. The philosopher now found himself faced with the question: Is it true? Does a supernatural reality exist? Are there gods and goddesses? Is there a rational foundation for accepting the divine?

Among the Greek philosophers it was Aristotle (384–322 B.C.) who gave lasting form to the logical argument for God's existence. He started from the observed fact of change. Things in this world continuously change and this change is best exemplified in locomotion. Aristotle argues as follows: if a thing is moved, it is either moved by itself or by something else. For instance if a stone is moved, it may be moved by a stick. If we consider this stick, it again can either be moved by itself or by something else. In this case it may be that the stick is moved by my hand. Now, if I consider a human being, I can ask again whether that human being is moved by himself or by something else. Well, it is clear that human beings themselves also undergo changes and are, therefore, moved by something else. If we consider reality in this fashion, we see that there are chains of things moved by other things. A moved object is moved by a mover, but the mover itself is again moved by another mover. Like this we have a succession of moved movers. Now, Aristotle points out, it is impossible that this chain or succession of moved movers be an infinite chain. Somewhere we should reach a *"first mover"*, an agent that itself is not moved but which can move other things.

Suppose that we see a chain hanging from a wall. The

118

lowest link will be suspended from the link above it. This link will again be supported by the link above it. Like this, one link will depend upon the other, but finally we should reach the link that is nailed to the wall, and from which the whole chain is suspended. Similarly, if secondary causes exist, which in turn cause one another, but are themselves caused by other secondary causes, we must eventually accept the existence of a First Cause that is not caused itself but that causes everything else.[123]

We could put Aristotle's argument in this way: the world we see requires a Cause. But this cause must itself be different from the world (and therefore not be caused itself) otherwise it could not be the ultimate cause of the world. This argument returns in many forms with all the old philosophers of different civilizations. If one sees a statue hewn out of rock, one knows that it was made by a craftsman. Likewise, if we study the world, we know that it was made by God. The Book of Wisdom (100 B.C.) states:

> For all those who are ignorant of God are foolish by nature. For they are unable from the good things that are seen to know him who exists. Neither do they recognize the craftsman while paying heed to his works. . . For from the greatness and beauty of created things we can, by comparison, understand their Creator (Wisdom 13:1, 5).

Philo of Alexandria (20 B.C. – A.D. 54) uses the comparison of a city. Anyone who enters a city and sees its buildings can understand that it has been built by human beings, he says. On observing the order and the planning that must have gone into the construction, one can deduce that some competent ruler has been the king of the city. Similarly, Philo says, when we study nature, how well-ordered it

119

is, with light during the day and food for all living beings, we can understand that the world too must have had someone who was "the Father and Creator and Governor of all these systems". "For there is no artificial work whatever which exists of its own accord. And the world is the most perfect of all works."[124]

God and being

In the Indian Nyaya and Vaisesika schools of philosophy there was much argumentation about the proof of God's existence from causality. Traditional Indian philosophy stated: "Whoever sees a pot, knows there must have been a potter. So whoever sees the world knows there must have been a Creator." The Buddhist thinker Dharmakirthi (A.D. 600–660) did not agree with this argument. He explained his reason why.

When we find an earthen pot we can prove that there must have been a potter who made it. But we can only draw this conclusion because we have seen other potters make pots. A person who has never seen other potters mould pots might, for instance, conclude that an ant-hill is also made by a potter. In this same way, although we have seen craftsmen make smaller things, no one has ever seen God making the universe. As this direct experience is lacking, we cannot prove God from looking at the universe alone. Our argument is not complete.

The best answer to Dharmakirthi's objection was given by Trilocana (about A.D. 800). He formulated his reply in words such as the following:

The objection is based on the assumption that our argument from causality needs to rest on factual

120

observation. However, this is not true. Our mind has the power to deduce from the observation of external facts qualities that belong to the *being* of objects. From observing the way in which pots are made by potters, our mind does not only stop at the external reality, but can draw conclusions about common qualities which we always find present in pot making. For example, the mind grasps that every pot depends on a potter. This quality of pots is not something accidental, but a thing that belongs to their nature, their being (*svabhava*). The dependence of a pot on a potter is its relationship or dependence of being (*svabhavikah sambandhah*).

Now, observing many instances of potters making pots is certainly helpful to focus attention on this dependence. But is it necessary? No. One case by itself would suffice. Because, if we study a pot well, we can observe that it must have been made by someone; we can see its "dependence of being". Our grasp of this fundamental principle is verified even in one particular case. The same happens when we study the universe. "We haven't seen God and we have not seen gods creating other universes. Yet, looking at reality surrounding us we can see in its very essence a *dependence of being* that points to an Original Cause"[125]

As Trilocana demonstrates, the argument from casuality is linked to the question of being. This leads us to consider the necessity of the Creator and the contingency of created beings.

Suppose that a certain Pandit Rao has a palm tree in his garden. No other palm tree in the world is quite the same. Yet there are some general qualities in it which we find also in other things. Pandit Rao's palm is a "tree" like many other trees. It is "tall" like a house or a church tower. It is "living" like grass, insects, buffaloes and men.

Pandit Rao's palm tree is also a "material object" like a rock, a beam of iron or a lorry. General qualities such as "trees", "tall", "living", and "material objects" are called *universals* because they do not name one individual object but denote a universal quality observable in many objects.

If we study the universals that we use, we find they are of two kinds. Some are *univocal* because the quality does not admit of degrees. A certain thing either is a tree or it is not; it cannot be more tree or less tree. Other universals are *analogous*, that is, they apply more to one object than to another. A church spire can be taller than a tree. Man can be said to be more living than a tuft of grass. When we apply an analogous universal, we know that it is partly true and partly false. A tuft of grass is living in as far as it can grow and propagate itself. But it is not living in as far as it cannot see or understand.

The most universal quality we find in things is the predicate of "being". Man "is", a buffalo "is", a tree and a tuft of grass "are". "Being" is obviously an analogous universal, because grass, animals and people have being in different degrees. In fact, it is this analogy of being that makes our thinking and speaking possible. When I say "the cat is alive", I am really saying that the cat has being in as far as it has life. We use the predicate "being" to connect names with universals ("John is a teacher") and to connect universals with one another ("Teachers are learned").

The necessary Being

If we take our starting point from the discovery that everything has "being", and if we think of the origin of all the different kinds of beings we find in the world, our mind is naturally led to accept one, necessary, always-existing, infinite Being from which all other beings derive their existence. In the Chandogya Upanishad (VI.2,2; 8,6) we read:

> In the beginning, my dear, there was Being alone,
>   one only without second.
> Some people say: "In the beginning there was *non-being* alone, one only, without second.
> From that non-being, being was produced."
> "But how, indeed, my dear, could it be thus?"
>   said he.
> How could being be produced from non-being?
> On the contrary, my dear,
> In the beginning there was *Being* alone,
>   one only, without second.
> All these creatures, my dear,
>   have their root in Being.
> They have Being as their abode,
>   Being as their support.[126]

Thomas Aquinas (1224–74) developed the same argument in this way:

> We find in nature things that can exist or not exist, since they are found to be generated and to be corrupted; and consequently, it is possible for them to be or not to be. But it is impossible for these always to exist, for that which can not-be, at some time is not. Therefore, if everything can not-be, then at one time there was nothing in existence, because that which does not exist begins to exist only through something already existing. Therefore, if at one time nothing was in existence, it would have been impossible for anything to have begun to exist; and thus even now nothing would be in existence. . . which is absurd. Therefore, not all beings

123

are merely possible, but there must exist something the existence of which is necessary.

But every necessary thing either has its necessity caused by another, or not. Now it is impossible to go on to infinity in necessary things which have their necessity caused by another, as has been already proved in regard to efficient causes. Therefore we cannot but admit the existence of some Being having of itself its own necessity, and not receiving it from another, but rather causing in others their necessity. This all people speak of as God.[127]

We see that in this argument two conclusions are reached. First of all, the existence of God is established. Secondly, it is deduced that God must be infinite and different from all created beings. The same thought was developed extensively in Muslim thought. From the contingent beings of this world (things that could be or could not be) the existence of one supreme Creator can be known. This Creator cannot resemble any created things. Ibn Tumart stated in A.D. 1103:

If it is known that Allah is the Creator of everything, it is known also that he does not resemble anything, since a thing resembles only what is of its own species. The Creator — glory be to him — cannot possibly be of the species of created things, for had he been of that species he would have been incapable with their incapacities.[128]

It should be noted that the validity of this argument in support of the existence of God depends on the analogy of being. From the imperfect way in which the world "is" we deduce the perfect way in which God "is". Actually we cannot see God's being nor fully understand it. Yet using the term "being" in an analogous way we can say "God is" with some real meaning. We know that what we say is partly true and partly false. It is partly true, because God in some real sense "is" as things in the world are. It is partly false because God has this being in an infinite sense, a sense in which we cannot predicate it of anything we know.[129]

With all these discussions we are really in the thick of metaphysical thinking. With their need of clear frameworks, of structures and closely-knit models, the city builders of the Indus valley, of Greece and of Medieval Europe had also constructed mental patterns of the universe in which God was the linchpin. Without the support of his creative Being everything would collapse, they thought; but their precise mental constructions were severely challenged by the thinkers of our modern age as we shall see in the next chapter.

15

The Search for a Phantom Gardener

After seeing *Star Wars* or another movie on extra-terrestrial space, one needs a few minutes to adjust to the real world. We can so easily immerse ourselves in a world of total fancy. For some time, purely fictitious people, objects and events appear to be real. Leaving the cinema we pinch ourselves, and look dazedly at familiar scenes in the street, realizing that our exploits in outer space were just imagination. If we do not bring ourselves down to our contemporary pavement, with both feet firmly on it, we may well be run over by a bus.

It seems to me that philosophers run a similar danger. By their speculation and abstraction the metaphysicians of the Middle Ages created a world of their own in which it was difficult to discern what was real, what was not. The danger was even greater when they talked about God who, by their own definition, in any case lay beyond the mind's full grasp. The result has been centuries of intellectual reasoning and counter-reasoning that have left most people confused. Since our thinking about God is still in many ways influenced by the old polemics, I want to present in a nutshell what the argument was all about.

Anselm of Canterbury (1033-1109) deserves to be called

the arch-metaphysician of Europe. He formulated the most daring logical proof for God ever put into words. For him, everything should be judged from God's point of view, not the other way about. If God is God, then he *must* exist; it is simply part of his definition.

Whereas the classical argument for God's existence took its beginning from the factual world, Anselm's argument starts from the *idea* of being. It became known as the "ontological proof". Put in a nutshell, its reasoning comes to this: The very fact that I can *think* of the most perfect being proves that it exists. Because, if it could not exist in my thought, I could not have the most perfect idea of being. Therefore, if it *must* have existence even in my thought, it must also exist in reality.

For it is one thing for an object to be in my mind, another for me to know that the object exists. When a painter conceives an idea of what he will put on canvas, he has it in his mind, but does not yet know it to exist because he has not yet executed it. But after finishing the painting he both has it in his mind and he knows that it exists because he has made it.

Now even a fool must admit that he has in his mind the notion of the greatest being (God) that could possibly be thought of. Because when we tell him about it, he grasps the idea. And when he grasps an idea, it has a place in his mind. But here we get the contradiction. Surely the greatest being that could possibly be thought of cannot exist in the mind alone. For if it existed in the mind alone, then we could think of it as existing in reality; and the latter would be greater. This would mean that if the greatest being that could possibly be thought of, exists in the mind alone, we could think of something greater than this greatest being that could possibly be thought of. But obviously this is impossible.

Hence, there is no doubt that there exists the greatest being that could possibly be thought of. It exists both in our mind and in reality.[130]

It does not require a genius to see that Anselm's argument is not valid. However much he may argue about the necessity for the idea of God to include its existence, he may not, from the mental "idea" of God, conclude that God really exists. Anselm actually maintains that the idea of the existing God is self-evident; it needs no other proof than the idea itself. It is self-evident that "every woman is a human being" because the predicate "human being" is implicitly contained in the subject "every woman". But when we say: "God exists", the predicate "exists" is not self-evident of God, because we do not know God directly. His existence or non-existence is not obviously implicit in our idea of God, but must be proved from actual beings. In short: the fact that something exists in our mind does not prove that it exists in reality. This also applies to the idea of God.[131]

Battles of the mind

Today most philosophers outside the mainstream religions reject the metaphysical argument for God's existence. Their reasons are: the believer argues from his own ideas to facts which he cannot observe; the law of causality may not apply to the whole universe as such; belief in God cannot be verified or falsified; evolution has proved that the universe can explain itself.

Many of these objections were formulated first by David Hume (1711-76), but it is through Kant (1724-1804) in particular that they have come to be almost universally accepted.

Immanuel Kant held that the metaphysical argument for God's existence, as it was used by Thomas Aquinas, depends on the ontological argument and is, therefore, equally invalid. The argument from contingent being, Kant said, has two parts: first one argues from unnecessary beings to the existence of a necessary being; then one deduces that this necessary being must be infinite and perfect. The first part of the argument is based on experience and leads to some kind of valid conclusion. From the contingent beings in the world we can deduce that there must be some cause which is not of the same contingency. The second step, however, leading us from the necessary to the perfect being is, according to Kant, a disguised form of the ontological argument. For in this part of the argument we are no longer in touch with observable objects, but from *the idea* of the non-contingent being, we argue to the *fact* of an infinite and perfect being outside our observable world.[132]

Kant stated that it is impossible for us to demonstrate God's existence in this way because we are caught in the categories of our own mind. Our intellect is based on the perception of sense knowledge. Once we move outside the realm of our observable categories our thinking becomes purely speculative, "self-made", subjective, unverifiable and consequently unreal. If God is outside and above our earthly reality (as we presume when we call him infinite), he falls outside the scope of our valid human argument. "God is a fancy of the mind", said Dennis Diderot (1713-84). "If you want me to believe in God, you must make me *touch* him."

The Thomistic philosophers of our century have made gallant efforts to defend the validity of the metaphysical approach to God. Everything hinges on a correct understanding of *analogy*, they say. Kant would be right in rejecting the metaphysical argument if this could be claimed to lead to an idea of God such as we have of other persons or objects which we have experienced. As we have no direct experience of God we can have no positive idea of him. We only have an *analogous* idea of God, an idea constructed from comparison with other things that we do have ideas of. I cannot have a positive idea of my own death or of myself flying in outer space, because I have not experienced them. But from what I know of other people dying or flying in space I can have an analogous idea of what my death or my participation in a space programme would mean. This analogous idea is limited, of course (or, "partly wrong"), but that does not mean that it is totally useless or totally false. In the same way the idea we build up about God as the necessary being derives from our knowledge of other beings. The idea is very limited and partly distorted, no doubt, but still it contains a valuable kernel of truth.[133]

Kant's objection could also be put like this: the principle of causality holds good in our world, in the world which we can observe; we may not, without evidence, apply this principle to reality outside this world. From causality "within" the world we may not legitimately conclude that there is a causality "outside" the world. They are two different logical spheres. Bertrand Russell (1872-1970) illustrated it in this way: every human being who exists has a mother, but this does not mean that the *whole human race* should have a mother. Similarly although we can say that *within* the universe one thing is next to another, or over or below other things, we could never say that the universe itself is next to something else. It belongs to a different category in which the same principles that affect inner–universe objects are no longer valid. From the fact that objects within the universe are caused by one another we may not conclude that the whole universe as such is caused by something else.[134]

The Thomists have an answer to this objection too. "What you say is true of individual objects and their mathematical totals", they would say. "Even though every

130

person has a mother, it does not follow that the added totality of all human beings has a mother. Even though every soldier wears a helmet, it does not mean that the whole army as such wears a helmet. But our question does not concern the mathematical totality of beings but the depth and totality of *being* as such."

"Your argument", they would continue, "really means this: About things *within* the universe we may and can ask questions, but not about the universe as such. But this is surely illogical. For the philosophical question regarding the origin of being and order is nothing else but going deeper than mere physical or biological questions.

"Let me give you an example. Suppose a railway accident has happened. A train has run off the rails and many people have been killed as a result. The committee of investigation may find out that the cause of the accident lay in the engine driver going too fast round a bend. The investigation could stop there. But the committee might also carry on to ask deeper and more general questions: 'How sharp are the curves in our railway lines? What is the maximum safe speed at which trains can travel when taking those bends? Have sufficient safety measures been taken?' These questions do not concern trains as a mathematical totality (all trains together can't fly off a curve!), but as a totality of *being*.

"Questions about the totality of being are very useful and can be answered", they would conclude. "The causality of a more fundamental mistake underlies the particular causality of one accident. The causality of being as such must underlie the causality of particular things within the universe."[135]

No falsification?

Another way of putting Kant's objection has been expressed

131

by Anthony Flew. He says that we can prove the metaphysical argument wrong because it cannot be "falsified". In modern science it is generally accepted that every proof must be such that anyone could handle the same proof, either proving it to be correct (by verification) or proving it to be wrong (by falsification). The demonstration that a molecule of water contains two hydrogen atoms can be verified or falsified by any competent person. But what philosophers say about God, the necessary, infinite and perfect being, can neither be verified nor falsified. "What evidence should there be", Flew says, "for the metaphysician to accept that there is *no* God?"

Flew devised a parable in which he illustrates this. Two explorers come to a patch in a forest where many plants grow and flourish. "This plot is tended by a gardener", says one (the metaphysician). "There is no gardener", maintains the other (the scientist). They watch day and night to see whether a gardener comes. They notice nothing. "But perhaps he is an invisible gardener." They put up a barbed wire fence, use bloodhounds and try every possible means, but still they find no trace of the gardener, and the plants keep growing. But the metaphysician continues to maintain: "There *is* a gardener, but he cannot be seen, felt, touched, smelt or heard. Invisibly he comes and tends his garden." The scientist then exclaims: "What can I do to falsify your statement about the gardener? How is your invisible, intangible, eternally elusive gardener different from an imaginary gardener or no gardener at all?"[136]

Thomists answer this objection, pointing out that every argument should be verified or falsified in its own way. In physics, proofs which rest on experimental observation should be proved right or wrong by the same kind of observation. But philosophical arguments, which are based on logic and the grasp of being, can only be accepted or

132

rejected in terms of the same logic and reason. "It is stupid", they would contend, "to try to *see* an invisible gardener! Moreover, if we were to compare the First Cause with a gardener, we should certainly not think of his care for the garden in terms of external actions such as pruning or pouring water. As the First Cause he establishes the plants in their being, and this dependence cannot be demonstrated or falsified by putting up barbed wire or keeping bloodhounds."

For many scientists the fact of evolution has become another reason for rejecting the metaphysical proof of God's existence. Evolution seems to imply that a Creator is no longer needed. A scientist such as Gordon Childe (1882-1957) would explain his point of view as follows:

> The proof for God's existence rests on the assumption that the universe depends on something outside itself for its order and being. However, this assumption is unfounded. Modern science has demonstrated that *the universe can explain itself.*
>
> We can show how from very simple atomic material the universe slowly connected into stars and galaxies. We can prove that life and the higher forms of beings arose *through evolution.* We can follow the path of development from the formation of the first chemical molecules to the first living cells in the ocean, and then up the ladder of plant and animal life. Even man himself and his power of thinking and dominating the world can be explained by natural growth. There is no need to accept a Creator. Man made himself.[137]

Believing scientists do not find it difficult to counter this line of thinking. Teilhard de Chardin (1881-1955) was both an eminent palaeontologist and a theologian. He maintained that an evolved world needs a creator all the more. "Both evolution and the balance of matter", he would say, "increase rather than diminish the necessity of accepting a creator. They have underlined as never before the absolute submission of matter to the higher principles that govern it.[138]

"What do you mean when you say that the world 'can explain itself'? Let us take an example. The reasons for the working of a thermometer are in the thermometer itself: if the temperature rises, the mercury will automatically expand. A living seed will, in favourable circumstances, naturally grow into a plant. In this sense it explains itself. But in another sense neither the thermometer nor the plant can explain itself, because they cannot understand their own operation (they have no mind), nor could they bring themselves about (they are contingent beings)."

It is difficult to evaluate correctly the present state of the debate, but some kind of stalemate has been reached. Both Thomists and Kantians speak their own language. Both sides make a valid contribution to our search for God—the Thomists by insisting that we can say something meaningful about God; the Kantians by pointing out that discussing God or inner-world objects involves different thought processes, and that these cannot simply be equated. God is not an object in the world. It would seem that the deadlock can only be broken by a fresh approach to the problem such as is presented in functional thinking.

16

Prayer in
the Stock Exchange

I have a friend who is a stockbroker, one of the most matter-of-fact and practical people I have ever known. One day Harry, for that is his name, took me to the Stock Exchange in Throgmorton Street, London, to show me how it worked. This was before the "Big Bang" of computer dealing. "'Jobbers' who specialize in certain stocks and shares have their own 'pitch' on the floor of the Stock Exchange", Harry explained to me. "The jobbers 'make' prices for each share by offering a buying and selling price. Brokers strike a deal when the price is right for the investors they are representing."

As Harry was talking, I noticed that his attention was drawn to excitement in one corner of the Exchange. We got nearer and looked at the huge tables displaying the trend of buying and selling. Suddenly Harry's face grew pale. "My God", he said. "Lighthouse Aluminium [or some such firm] has fallen thirty pence!" As we watched, the price fell even lower. "Oh dear God, stop this!", I heard him murmur. "Please, don't let it happen. . ." It turned out that he had bought thirty thousand shares for a client on the previous day, in the firm conviction that it was a secure investment.

Later in a nearby pub I challenged him. "I heard you say a prayer", I stated. "'Dear God, stop this!', or something to the same effect. Do you really think God will listen to such a request?"

He looked thoughtful for some time. "In my work I need God, you know", he said. "But it is difficult to see what I really meant. I wasn't asking for a miracle really. It was some expression of worry, I suppose; of dependence. I believe prayers like that should not be taken on their content value, but on what they express in another way."

He paused a while and then said: "I suppose it's like money. A banknote is just a piece of paper with little intrinsic worth. But it's worth a lot by what it can do."

Judging things by what they can do is characteristic of functional thinking. And that, for better or for worse, is the kind of thinking we have become used to today. Before we can discuss the effect this has on our concept of God, it may well be necessary to reflect on the origin of this manner of thinking: survival in urban surroundings.

Urbanized Life

Modern technology has changed the township of former centuries into the city of today. Urbanized society is not just different from township society in the number of people living together or in other quantitative aspects. The quality of life and the inner structure of human relationships have been profoundly altered.[139]

The secular city of today is not a "community" but *a network of functional relationships*. In a township society people had different professions, but these professions were not the basis on which relationships in the community were built. In urbanized life the opposite is true. An urban citizen meets hundreds of people every day, but mainly in their professional capacity: the ticket collector, the waiter, the

136

clerk in the bank, the customer, the policeman. He could not possibly have a deep personal acquaintance with them. He does not need to know their name, their home background or their religion. Social life in the city will only work if these many relationships are maintained on a strictly functional level. Of course, a city man will have some personal friends, but the very structure of city life makes it necessary to restrict their number. He could not possibly begin close acquaintance with all the persons attending his school or working in his factory or travelling with him on the Underground.

In urbanized society *communication* too has taken on new dimensions. It is manifold, fast and public. In townships, people used to pick up rumours at the local teashops, on the market or at unofficial gatherings. News was carried by word of mouth. Contacts were made face to face. Communication was with people one knew. The citizen of today is constantly speaking to people he cannot see— by telephone, by the microphone or by correspondence. He is continuously being addressed by persons who do not know him—through the newspapers, the radio, the film and television. He knows what is going on in society and he is in unceasing and multiple contact with it. But communication tends to be functional and not addressed to him as an individual.

City life is extremely *mobile*. It is enough to watch traffic in the peak hour between eight and nine in the morning to see the implications. Everyone in the city is constantly on the move—to one's place of work, to shopping areas, to one's home, to places of entertainment. The whole commerce and traffic of the city are constructed to allow for this multiple interchange of places, for this moving of crowds in all directions at the same time. City life presupposes adaptability. If one shop is closed another will be open. If one job is lost, another job in some other firm must be accepted. The traditional pattern of the stable home with the inherited trade cannot survive.

Urbanized society is *achievement-orientated*. What counts for survival and making a living is not one's own likings or beliefs, but success. The article that is bought by many people proves to be a good product: factories and shopkeepers will model their trade to supply it. Skills in demand are rewarded with good salaries; however praiseworthy in themselves, talents that are not experienced as useful will find no means of subsistence. The houses, shops, banks, work places and schools are designed to afford the maximum output of utility. The outlook of city people is necessarily pragmatic. The question is not: What is the intrinsic value of this or that? but: What is its use? Will it work? Is it practical?

Another feature of modern society is that it is *secularized*. What we mean by this is that in the various aspects of its organization the causality of religion is consciously and on principle excluded. When treating patients in a hospital the doctor is not supposed to do faith healing or recite mantras: he has to diagnose the disease and give medical treatment as if God did not exist. The policeman who is investigating a murder may not spend his time in a temple praying for a divine revelation. He is expected to gather evidence and pursue the criminal as if God did not exist. The same applies to all other professions: the nurse, the mechanic, the schoolmaster, the bus conductor, the accountant. All have their own specific tasks which they have to fulfil in accordance with professional and scientific norms. To the modern citizen his or her allegiance to a particular religion or personal belief does not enter one's function or profession in society. Whatever people may believe as individuals, society as such is organized as if God does not exist.[140]

138

Pragmatic truth

The process of changing from a township to a secular society is still going on. It is further advanced in some countries, retarded in others. The important thing for us to note is that the changeover also implies the new way of thinking which has been called *functional thinking*. It can be called a "new way of thinking" because it entails a fundamental difference in the understanding of life and reality. The philosopher of past ages tried to see how persons and objects fitted into some kind of totality of truth. The pragmatist of secular society tries to understand how persons and objects function in the immediate context of his world. This is not an attempt to deny the larger reality or to reduce objective truth to subjective utility. It is simply that the citizen of today has come to realize the relativity of general concepts and the necessity of tackling problems within a manageable scope.

An example may illustrate the difference in approach. A traditional Christian who lived, let us say, in 1900, found it difficult to join a Muslim colleague in a prayer service. The underlying reason was the approach of "total truth" implied in metaphysics. The Christian felt that he could not join the Muslim without first checking on the whole faith of Islam. He felt that the condition of error which he had to hold the Muslim to be in, somehow affected everything the latter did. Also, the Muslim's prayer was the prayer of an "unbeliever". Moreover, his own participation in the Muslim service would to some extent involve the whole Christian Church, he thought. It seemed impossible to him to join his colleague in prayer unless some fundamental principles and general truths had first been agreed upon.

We see here how universal concepts dominated his thinking: error, the whole Church, heresy, Christianity,

Islam, etc. The secular, functionally thinking Christian will exclude such general concepts as irrelevant to the particular problem of his joining the prayer service. Whether Christianity or Islam is the right religion has no bearing on this problem. What other beliefs the Muslim has does not concern him *here and now*. In fact, it seems of little importance whether he is a Muslim, a Buddhist or a Hindu. For this particular, limited problem of whether he should pray together with his colleague, the urbanized Christian feels he only needs to consider if it has a function and if it is justified in the immediate context of their relationship. Probably he will find that the proposed common prayer is extremely meaningful, and will then decide to join without feeling the need of settling many questions of theoretical truth and general principle.

Language Games and God-talk

To express what we think we use language. In the past it has been taken for granted that our words correspond to concepts and these concepts to objects. Truth meant that the statement in human language and outside reality agree; falsehood that they do not agree. All language was taken in an objectivistic sense. In fact, philosophers of the past simply forgot about language, just as writers today do not think it worthwhile to reflect on the pens they hold or the typewriters or word processors they use.

In our time we have discovered that language is a much more complicated tool than this. If I say: "Prabhat Singh is your opponent", it gives a different message in different circumstances. It could be that I am sportsmaster and hereby telling you that I appoint Prabhat Singh to oppose you in a game of tennis. It may also be that I am giving you information about who your opponent is in an election campaign. I may also be a police instructor who is presenting an imaginary case to pupils in a detective school. The precise meaning of what we are saying can only be determined from a knowledge of the activity we are engaged in. Linguistic analysts call a whole set of human actions taking place in a particular context and having its own specific symbols and expressions a *language game*.[141]

The businessman, the journalist, the politician, the scientist, the housewife, the college student: each uses his or her own "language game" with its specific rules and meanings. For judging the truth and validity of a statement we have to judge it within its own language game. When the farmer says: "Bob is my shepherd", it has decisively a different meaning than in the believer's prayer: "The Lord is my shepherd."

Linguistic analysis was taken up first by English scientists. On account of their empirical training they were inclined to take scientific object-language as the norm of relevance. Ordinary language, they maintained, can be verified or falsified by direct observation. Only such object-language as "There John comes riding a bicycle" is obviously meaningful. The metaphysical use of language falls outside empirical observation, and was therefore ruled out as having only secondary meaning. The word "God", they said, was an artificial and meaningless word, because it could not be verified.

At first sight it looks as if the advance of knowledge proves these linguists right. God is not a causality within the world. It is nonsense to think of God as one doctor among so many others, or of his blessing as a healing drug competing with penicillin in effectiveness. *Within* the science of medicine God does not exist: it is not correct to ascribe illnesses and cures to some kind of miraculous intervention by God in human life. God does not belong to the language game of science.

But this does not mean that the word "God" is not

141

very meaningful in other spheres of human language. Many valid aspects of our human existence fall outside the immediate scope of scientific observation. The scientist who makes a new discovery may be jumping with joy in his laboratory. But the experience of joy or sadness are typically *human* experiences that cannot be defined in descriptive scientific terms. Science can analyse the inner composition of sound in a spectrograph — but it cannot judge the beauty of a melody, it cannot appreciate paintings, sculpture and architecture, as an intelligent person can do. Most of all, science cannot judge the moral value of its inventions. Science can produce nuclear explosives, but it requires responsible human beings to decide in what circumstances they may be used. Human beings are persons, and as such much greater than science. They show in their lives an involvement in reality that goes beyond descriptive object language.

Further probes

Some theologians have explained the meaningfulness of God in terms of ethics. According to them "God" is part of the human language game of moral responsibility. By speaking of God the creator of all and supreme judge of all our actions, we are expressing our dependence on other beings and the need to subordinate our aims to the common good. The kind of language we use when we speak of God is the language of "parable", they say. We speak of God as if he is our "Father", who "sees us", who "leads us on the right path", etc. When employed in religious language these expressions do not have their face value, but express some other reality in a transferred sense.[142]

If this is understood as though the reality of God is nothing else but human ethics, the approach is obviously inadequate. We have then reduced God to a mere fiction. He would have no reality apart from his role in human society, and thus he would exactly be the opposite of what we want to express by the term "God". But many philosophers speak of religious language as the language of parable in a much more positive sense. They are convinced that God is a true *reality*, even though he is not an *object* in the world in which we live.

As our human language is based on this object-world, we can only apply its terms to God in a transferred sense. In religious "language of parable" we employ every-day terms, but remember that they have a different meaning when applied to God. When I say: "God sees me and watches over me every moment of the day", I know that these terms are not true of God in the object sense of the words. God has no eyes, he does not move through time, and he is simply not like any other object or person in our world. But I know that the statement expresses something valuable to me. It is like a parable. It conveys God's relationship to me in the image of a watchful father.

As these developments in linguistic philosophy are rather recent, it is difficult to survey them accurately. Moreover, it is not easy at this moment to discern what is passing and what will be of lasting value. One thing seems certain: many philosophers are making the discovery that the language game of religion has an objective basis. From among the various new lines of thought I would like to single out two that seem to me of special importance.

Linguistic analysis shows that human communication is taking place at more levels at the same time. There is a communication of contents and a communication of relationship. The second is called meta-communication. If I say: "Please have lunch with me tomorrow", I am inviting someone to lunch (the contents), but by the words I choose, by my attitude and facial expression, I am at the same time conveying that this invitation is an expression of

143

friendship (relationship). Sometimes we also express meta-communication in words, for instance when we say: "It would mean a lot to me." Underlying this second level of communication there is again a deeper level by which we express our general attitude to ourselves and to others (e.g. "I try to understand others; I like people"). And below this over-all relationship level there is a fourth level, closely related to the fundamental position of our personality regarding existence as such (in the line of "I'm OK. I'm happy to exist").

Each of these four levels of communication is real. Human language, however, developed particularly in view of first-level communication. It is geared to be useful in the accurate transfer of informational messages. Using human language to explicate what is going on in second-, third- or fourth-level communication is progressively more difficult if not utterly impossible. Language simply cannot do the job. Religion, these linguists point out, lies on the fourth level of communication as it concerns our basic attitude to ourselves, to existence and reality. The difficulty of religious language arises from our attempt to express our real experience of fourth-level communication in terms of first-level content language.[143]

Other philosophers start from the reality of religious experience itself. The essence of a genuine religious experience, they say, is a flash of insight and commitment by which we are brought face to face with ultimate reality. Religion makes use of descriptive language in which people talk about God and realities related to him, as if they are objects of our day-to-day world. But these "words about God" are only the launching pad from which our religious experience can take off. In genuine religious language the descriptive meaning of the word is transcended by a "cosmic disclosure" in which a person suddenly understands an aspect of ultimate being and surrenders himself or herself to it. If I exclaim: "God, my God, why have you forsaken me?", I am using descriptive language (complaining like a child left by his father), but through these words I may experience a "disclosure situation", a break-through to the reality of God.[144]

In recent years science itself has made unexpected discoveries about the nature of the world. The new questions raised seem to touch religion almost directly in their search for meaning. How do space, matter and existence relate? What existed before the Big Bang? What will exist after the universe collapses? How can consciousness influence physical entities? How come that "the uncertainty principle", quantum jumps, and the anthropocentric thrust of evolution agree with mystic and religious views? Many scientists are searching for a more functional approach in their own discipline that would allow for a holistic understanding of reality and thus include God.[145]

Language is an instrument, a tool, a means we use for a variety of purposes. To understand what is happening we should go beyond the obvious, external impressions created by words and ask: "What is their function in this particular context?" Speaking about God and religious values is extremely meaningful. It need not in any way contradict the use of object language in other spheres of life.

17

The Way in
to "Grasping" God

Philosophers and theologians, mystics and saints are
unanimous in giving us this advice: "Realize that in his
deepest mystery God remains unknowable. Negations about
him are often more correct than assertions. Rid your mind
of silly prejudices. Images say more about him than
intellectual notions. You come closest to God in a kind
of unknowing knowing." In short, their advice comes to
the following.

Always remember that God is far beyond what you can
say, think or imagine. He cannot be contained in your
human concepts. Lao Tzu stated: "The Tao that can be
put into words is not the eternal Tao." Al-Ghazali taught
that "it is impossible for anyone to understand God except
God". Thomas Aquinas agrees: "The ultimate reach of our
knowledge of God consists in realizing that we do not
know him. For then we grasp that what God *is* surpasses
all we *understand* of him."[146] You will never be able to
say you know God as he really is.

In practice this means that you are often on safer ground
denying imperfections about him than in making positive
assertions. In the ancient Indian Scriptures this is known
as: "Neti-neti"; "He is not this, he is not that". Do not

146

think it is useless to follow this path of negation. It will help you revere God to recall from time to time that he is not bound by such limitations as place, size, time, energy or range of vision.

In particular rid your mind of silly prejudices. He is just as much a mother as a father. He cannot really be happy one moment and angry the next; all his actions are one for all eternity. He is not more present high in the sky than anywhere else. Though for ever the same he is more act than object, more truly infinite dynamism than static royalty seated on a throne. Do not cheapen your concept of God. Purify your ideas constantly. Shake them loose.

Images, if they are understood to be just that and no more, can tell you more about God than intellectual notions. Compare this to your knowledge of ordinary people. You have seen their features. You have heard their voice. You have touched them and observed their behaviour in various circumstances. From these images you build up a characterization of their personalities. You know them as individuals; yet you could never express such knowledge in precise words. So it will be with God. You know him as the inner creator and the judge within you. You see glimpses of him in different experiences of life. You hear stories about him, and parables; you reflect on traditional titles. All these are images that help you get to know him — quite distinctly, but never precisely or exhaustively.

When you get really close and intimate to another person, you do not need to say much. Wordless communication begins to bind you in an unspeakable depth of love. This also applies to the way you know God—all the more so because he resides within you; because he is a deep well from which your life springs forth in silence. Knowing God in this mystical way is called "unknowing knowing"

147

since it is reached by stripping the mind of words, ideas and images. Ruysbroeck describes it in these terms:

> Pure not-knowing is the light in which one can see God. Those who experience this not-knowing feel as if they are in the desert even though God's light is there. Pure not-knowing surpasses human understanding but does not suppress it. . . It is in this unconditional not-knowing that one sees God, but without comprehending what one sees, for what is seen transcends all things.[147]

A good summary of the above advice may be seen in the following poem drawn up by a Christian monk in the sixth century. Read it slowly and meditatively to purify your notion of God. It is amazing how this statement of God's "otherness", if properly understood, expresses at the same time, paradoxically, the deepest grounds for his immanence. I especially commend the last paragraph to your prayerful consideration.[148]

> The cause of all things
>   embraces all
>   and is above all,
>   is not without being or without life.
>
> He does not lack reason or intelligence.
> Yet,
> he is not an object.
> He has no form or shape,
>   no quality, no quantity, no weight.
> He is not restricted to any place.
> He cannot be seen.
> He cannot be touched.
> Our sense cannot perceive him,
> our mind cannot grasp him.

He is not swayed by needs
  or drives
  or inner emotions.
Things or events that take place in our world
  can never upset him.
He needs no light.
He suffers neither change
  nor corruption nor divison.
He lacks nothing
and remains always the same.

He is neither soul nor intellect.
He does not imagine, consider, argue or understand.
He cannot be expressed in words
  or conceived in thoughts.
He does not fall into any category
  of number or order.
He possesses no greatness or smallness
  no equality or inequality
  no similarity or dissimilarity.
He does not stand, or move, nor is he addressed.

He does not yield power,
  neither is he power itself
  nor is he light.
He does not live
  nor is he life itself.
He may not be identified with being,
  nor with eternity or time.

He is not subject to the reach of the mind.
He is not knowledge,
  or truth,
  or kingship,
  or wisdom.

He is not the one, or oneness;
  not Godhead or goodness.
He is not even spirit
  in the way we understand it,
  or sonship or fatherhood.

He is not anything else known to us
  or to any other being.
He has nothing in common with things that exist
  or things that do not exist.
Nothing that exists
  knows him as he really is.
Nor does he know things that exist
  through a knowledge
  existing outside himself.
Reason cannot reach him,
  or know him.
He is neither darkness nor light,
  neither falsehood nor truth.

All statements affirmed about him
  or denied about him
  are equally wrong.
For although we can make positive or negative
  statements
  about all things below him,
We can neither affirm;
  nor deny him himself
  because the all-perfect and unique cause
  of all things
  is beyond all affirmation.
Moreover, by the simple pre-eminence
  of his absolute nature,
  he falls outside the scope
  of any negation.

He is free from every limitation
   and beyond them all.

The higher we rise in contemplation
   the more words fail.
Words cannot express pure mind.
When we enter the darkness
   that lies beyond our grasp
we are forced, not merely to say little,
   but rather to maintain an absolute silence,
   a silence of thought
   as well as of words. . .
As we move up from below
   to that which is higher
   in the order of being,
our power of speech decreases,
   until,
   when we reach the top,
   we find ourselves totally speechless.
We are then overcome
   by him who is wholly ineffable.

PART FOUR

THE MUSICIAN
IN OUR HEART

18

He Pitches His
Tent next door to Us

A Muslim teacher in India once talked to me about his search for truth. He had been an Imam in a small mosque until his congregation split on a matter of ritual orthodoxy. One of the issues was this: While leading prayers should the Imam hold his arms crossed in front of his chest? Or should he keep them on both sides of his body? The Imam, whom I will call "Ahmed", left his post when it dawned on him how people claimed to know "the Will of God" without any real evidence. It shook his faith in Islam.

"I decided to study other religions", he told me. "I spoke to Buddhists, Sikhs, Jains and Christians. I attended prayer services. I listened to scripture commentaries and sermons. I tried to follow the advice of various spiritual guides. I was like a man in a thick fog ready to join any passer-by in the hope that he would know the way. . ." As far as I know, Ahmed is still searching. Having lost his previous certainties, he has become a casualty of the world's religious confusion.

If we admit that we are walking in a fog, would it be so impossible to imagine God himself taking an interest and walking at our side? I know it sounds incredible; but then, are not life itself, and our individuality and so many other facts, incredible? If God is my origin and the source of my search, why would he not show his face to me in a more personal way?

155

So far I have spoken about God in somewhat general terms, but to do justice to the topic of this book that will not be enough. The time has come for me to share my deepest feelings and most personal experiences as a Christian. I want to explain why belief in God helps me, confirms me. I want to express how close I know him to be, in spite of my inability to understand him fully. I want to put into words why it is meaningful to me to be a Christian and not just a general believer. How shall I begin?

Fundamentalist Christians would probably expect me here to produce a "testimony", to narrate "how Jesus saved me". What I want to do is different. I am not comfortable in the company of fundamentalists, even if they are Christians. I respect their sincerity and admire their zeal. I am sure that my own experience agrees in essential points with theirs. Yet we are poles apart in other respects. I shudder at their contempt for the beautiful religious traditions outside Christianity. I cannot stand their overbearing certainties. I am suspicious of their charismatic enthusiasms and their scriptural literal-mindedness. I may well have found the same treasure that they have, but without losing my identity as a seeker, a man of this world, a realist — I hope — with both my feet on the ground.

God became human in Jesus Christ. Through Jesus he made himself known to us and offered us healing and love. Incredible though these beliefs may be, they are, I am convinced, absolutely true. And I know this not only because I possess rational proofs for them but because they give new meaning to my life. What I appreciate most of all is that, while God could only speak to me, heal me and love me in his reality as "the Other", he managed to do so "from within". Even in his transcendence he affirmed his immanence. Let me explain this more at length.

So far in this book we have focused on God as the origin

of everything we are, as the source from which we spring. We find God also in "otherness". Imagine I were to think, in presumption or plain stupidity, that the world belongs to me; that I can subject the whole of reality to my thought and influence. Soon I would find out my mistake. For the world proves to be different from what I might have thought or liked. I meet opposition, suffering, death. I meet other people who have their own needs and desires that vary from mine. I have to come to terms with this "otherness". It challenges me. If I pursue this "otherness" to its ultimate root, I find out that it can only be God, the origin of all individuality, the radically "other".[149]

I need "the other", because as long as I am thinking my own thoughts, I am speaking a monologue. Only when I meet "the other" do I enter into a dialogue and engage in direct contact with reality. Psychologists have shown that we need this dialogue for our full development. We need more than to experience participation with all reality through the warmth and security offered by *a mother* who caresses us and feeds us; we also need to meet the challenge of *a father* who speaks to us and makes demands. Facing us in "otherness" the father helps us discover our own identity in opposition to other realities in our world.[150]

There can be no doubt that our two most fundamental experiences of God — the immanent approach of oneness and the transcendent approach of autonomy — are based on these deep and early psychological stages of our development.[151] A healthy relationship to God requires both. The feeling of closeness we had to our mother, of snuggling against her and sucking her breast, released in us a basic capability for trust and mystical experience. Similarly, seeing our father's face and hearing his voice released in us the ability to act as an autonomous and yet responsible person. The contribution of the father is great:[152] it begins real human communication; it initiates the process of giving

157

and receiving mutual love; it offers the possibility of healing through reconciliation. It is only through an "I-Thou" relationship that we become fully human.[153]

Now, if such is the case it becomes plausible that God, if he is a god of love, should at some time or other make himself known in a "father function". What I mean is this: as the creator within us and the inner judge, God is somehow exercising his "mother function". We are comforted and reassured in feeling one with the source of all being. But if God wants me to discover my own identity as a person whom he loves, he could hardly leave my impressions about him to the "otherness" which I experience in this world. Though some people love me, others do not. Though some events bring me happiness, other ones sadden and discourage me. Left to myself I could not help but wonder what intentions God, "the other", has in my regard. This in turn would throw serious doubt on my own basic respectability and lovability as an autonomous person. To put it plainly: how will I ever know that God really loves me as a person, if he does not take the trouble to speak to me and say: "I love you!"?

And this is precisely what I, as a Christian, believe God has done. Through Jesus Christ he made himself known as a person interested in each one of us. He offers us healing and forgiveness — something we could never presume without his explicit assurance and explicit affirmation. He also tells us, what we might have guessed but could never know for certain, that he is love; that he invites us to a personal relationship.

> Love comes from God.
> Only the person who loves is a child of God
>   and knows God.
> Whoever does not love does not know God;
>   for God is love.
> 1 John 4:7-8

I stand at the door and knock.
If you respond to my voice and open the door,
I will enter your space and share your food;
and you will share with me.

Revelation 3:20

The whole of biblical revelation, starting from the Old Testament right through to its climax in Jesus Christ, proclaims this one exciting and meaningful message: God is not just a nondescript impersonal power; like me he is a person who knows and loves; he offers me his personal friendship.

Since he is infinity itself, eternal, utterly transcendent, what would have been more natural than to expect an overwhelming message "from above", a manifestation of stark power that would establish his "otherness" for good? Such, at least, would have been our human thinking. True to his own nature as the inner wellspring of all that exists, God chose a different path. Even while revealing his otherness, he wanted to approach us "from within". He did not want his word of revelation to contradict his immanent tenderness as creator. So what did he do? He spoke to me, healed me, loved me **as a human person.**

Some people have contended that incarnation, God-becoming-human, is no more than a religious dream. It originated in the fantasies and longings of human beings deprived of "human" contact with God, they tell us. And, in a manner of speaking, they are right. People *were* looking forward to an incarnation, as the history of various religions shows. It was natural for human beings reaching out to God to imagine that he would manifest himself to them in human form. But what could have remained just a dream, God turned into reality in a way no one could have

159

anticipated. Is this so strange, if we remember that it is God in the first place who inspires people's deepest religious longings?

The claim that Jesus Christ is God Incarnate must be substantiated with evidence; as I have done elsewhere.[154] What concerns me here is that, given such evidence, it becomes entirely plausible in the context of God's communication with humankind. Indeed, if he wanted to make himself known to us as someone who loves us and heals us, the way of the incarnation as believed in by Christians, makes excellent sense. In Jesus Christ, we believe, God himself shows his face. Both the real humanity of Jesus and the identification with God are required to make the belief tenable.

I say "identification with God" because only this renders the incarnation real. This is what the doctrine of the Divinity of Jesus entails. In him "the (eternal, uncreated) Word became a human being and pitched his tent among us, filled with grace and truth. We have seen his (divine) glory, glory as of the only-begotten Son of the Father" (John 1:14).

Jesus Christ,
though he was in the form of God,
did not reckon equality with God
    a thing to hold on to.
He emptied himself,
taking the form of a servant
by being born in the likeness of a human being.
And being found in human form,
he humbled himself even more
    and became obedient unto death,
even death on a cross.

                                    Philippians 2:6-8

Whatever Jesus said, was said by God. Whatever Jesus did, was God's doing. He was God among us (Matthew 1:23).

At the same time he was truly human. He had a spirit and a body as we have. He had to grow and learn, eat and drink, work and sleep, succeed and fail as we have to. He possessed all our weaknesses except sin (Hebrew 4:15). He shared our human fate of suffering and persecution. He even died a painful death at the hands of ruthless opponents. He could not have been more human, and yet it was precisely his human life that has become the most revealing and powerful image of God's love for us. It is the human Jesus who became the reflection of God's radiance on earth, the seal of God's nature (Hebrews 1:3). It was Jesus as a human person who was constituted Son of God in power (Romans 1:4).

> God made his love known to us by this that he sent his only Son into the world so that we might have life through him. Love did not come about by our love of God, but by his love of us and by his sending his Son to be healing for our sins.
>
> 1 John 4:9-10

> God showed his love for us in this that Christ died for us while we were yet sinners.
>
> Romans 5:8

> God so loved the world that he gave his only Son in order that whoever believes in him should not perish but have eternal life.
>
> John 3:16

For centuries people have looked at the incarnation as something from the outside; as they considered creation

161

and judgement. The incarnation was presented as God leaving his eternal, distant abode to step into our own small world. The concept was partly based on biblical imagery: Jesus came "from above" and "ascended again" to return to his Father. The vocabulary of his "coming" and "going" could so easily stress his other-worldly origin. But it is not the only, nor perhaps the most accurate, way of looking on the incarnation.

Suppose we approach the whole process from within? Suppose we see in God not the architect, but rather the inner soul and life-force that produced the whole universe? Everything that exists would exhibit some of the exuberance of his being: his beauty, his power, his unimaginable riches and splendour. God's own nature as knower and lover would shine forth even more clearly in human beings who carry his image in their spirit. Would it be so surprising if in the course of time this same ebullient, self-revealing God were to express his love and concern by investing one of those human beings with an overwhelming measure of himself? The incarnation, thus seen as God's special presence erupting within humankind, would be in line with God's progressive self-manifestation through creation. Though always remaining a free gift, the incarnation would complete and fulfil what he had already begun by causing created things to spring into existence.

This is what the New Testament actually teaches in the letter to the Colossians. Even though Jesus Christ appeared millions of years after the beginning of creation, he was there, in God's thoughts, from the start. He was the climax and summit of God's self-revelation. In him everything else God was doing in the universe would become meaningful.

Christ is the image of the invisible God,
the first-born heir of all creation.
For with a view to him all things were created,
in heaven and on earth,
visible and invisible,
whether thrones, powers, lords
or other spiritual authorities.
All things were created through him and for him.
He comes before all other things.
He is the head of his body, the Church.
He is the beginning,
the first to be risen from the dead,
that in everything he might be pre-eminent.
For in him all the fullness of God
was pleased to dwell.

Colossians 1:15-19

We should remember that this confession was written with our human earth in mind. To other intelligent creatures in distant parts of the universe God, the inner creator, may well have revealed himself in other climactic incarnations. To us, human beings, he revealed himself most fully through Jesus Christ. By doing so he respected our human autonomy. He spoke to us, healed us, loved us as one of us.

But how does the incarnation affect us? Does it give us newness of life? What does it consist in? Can we say that this new life too is something he creates in us from within? We will see about this in the next chapter.

19

His Spirit
Flows in Our Veins

Christianity is such a conglomeration of physical and social realities: of cathedrals, churches, schools and cemeteries; of hierarchies, feast days, customs and practices; of Bibles, prayer books, hymnals and missals; of sacraments, seminaries, symbols and synods. Yet none of such externals, necessary though they are to aid our human nature, constitutes the essence of Christianity. The essential reality, the thing that really matters, is what God does in our heart. "The kingdom of God is *within you*" (Luke 17:21). Since we are body as well as spirit, God meets us in images we can see, hear and touch. But the end result of God's action is an inner transformation that heals and sanctifies even the body, from within.

We Christians express this belief by saying that we have received God's Spirit. His Spirit lives in us. Through his Spirit we can think, feel, speak and act in a new way. Through the presence of this Spirit in us we know God in a new and intimate way. We feel strengthened and comforted, ready to undertake difficult tasks or endure severe trials. The Spirit of God makes us happy, optimistic, positive in our dealings with others. The Spirit helps us to be kind, understanding and patient. The Spirit teaches

164

us a whole new way of considering what is important and what is not.

The deepest roots of the Spirit in us lie in our created nature. If we reflect we will have detected in ourselves a longing for what is absolute, a reaching out to the infinite. Plato described this when he spoke of "eros", that natural love in us which seeks beautiful things but which ultimately can only be satisfied by the highest good.[155] Others have called it "the human capacity for creative self-transcendence",[156] or "the unrestricted open-ended quest".[157] It is clear, both from mystical experience and philosophical analysis, that both the origin and the goal of this dynamic thrust are ultimate reality, that is: God.[158] The mystics of all ages, whether Taoist, Hindu, Sufi, Christian or whatever tradition they belonged to, agree on this universal experience of the "Spirit". We have already spoken about this, though sometimes in different terms, in parts one and two of this book.

We Christians believe that Christ has brought us a heightened awareness of that same Spirit. Or rather: by re-creating us internally, Christ raised the activity of the Spirit in us to a higher level. This is sometimes expressed by saying that he gave us of his own Spirit. This spiritual activity, which is God's love in us, is his new law and the inner judge, as we saw in chapter ten. This new presence of God in us is the substance of Christian life. Its distinctive sign is the love kindled in our heart.

When the New Testament speaks of "love", it calls on the best in our human nature. Love means respect for the other, leading to selfless commitment. The love Jesus demands in the Gospel urges us to wash people's feet, feed the hungry, clothe the naked, nurse the sick, welcome strangers, visit prisoners and serve rather than expect to be served. If you love people with Christ's love, you tell the truth even if it embarrasses you; you forgive them

165

for their failings; you turn the other cheek rather than take revenge; you pray for those who curse you and persecute you. Christ's love opens our eyes so that we can love people for what they are; not for what we can get out of them. It requires us to make sacrifices, yes even to give our life if this be necessary.

"If you keep these commandments of my love," Jesus assured us, "I will make myself known to you" (see John 14:21). By practising Jesus's love we will have direct experience of him.[159] The love that we feel and practise is God's own doing in us. Through his love we are in direct touch with God himself. It is God who fills us with his love; who manifests his love to others through us.

> Love comes from God.
> Whoever practises love
>   is born of God and experiences God.
> Whoever does not practise love
>   has no experience of God.
> God is love.
>
> 1 John 4:7-8

> No one has ever seen God.
> But if we love one another,
>   God shows that he lives in us.
> Yes, it is his love that flourishes in us.
> By this we know
>   that God and we share the same life
> because he gives us his own Spirit (of love).
>
> 1 John 4:12-13

> God is love.
> He who lives full of love
>   lives full of God
> for it is God who fills him.
>
> 1 John 4:16

166

The implication of these texts is absolutely clear. When we strive to be fair and loving; when we try to be kind to others, defend their rights, treat them with respect, are willing to help them at some cost to ourselves, are patient and forgiving rather than spiteful — in short, when we try to live Jesus's commandment of love, we know that these feelings and actions flowing from us manifest the Spirit of God. We are not talking here of extraordinary deeds of self-sacrifice; we are speaking of our every-day efforts to be loving in our relationships. The remarkable message of sacred Scripture is that precisely such happenings in us disclose the presence of God to us.

God who created us in the first place, who gave us the capacity for transcending love to begin with, now through Christ strengthens our ability to be truly loving and constructive. Is it not a wonderful discovery to find out that this inner life in me, which I know so well because it is part of my every-day striving, is a tangible sign of God's presence in me?

Many Christians will know what I am talking about — from their own spiritual experience. Some who have lacked proper instruction or who have lost their way in the maze of externals, may wonder if I am only proclaiming a limited and personal interpretation of Scripture. For their benefit, allow me to expose how what I have said is precisely the teaching of St Augustine of Hippo, that eminent Doctor of the Church who left us so many standard classics of Christian theology (A.D. 354-430). Let us hear what he has to say.

> We know that God lives in us. How do we know it. . .? St John tells us: "Because he has given us of his Spirit." But how do we know that God *has* given us of his Spirit. . .? Search your heart. If it is full of love, you possess God's Spirit![160]

167

Perhaps, you will tell me: I haven't seen God. Will you tell me: I haven't seen a human person? Love your neighbour. If you love the neighbour you see, by this same act you will see God. For you will see love itself and God lives in love.[161]

Who doesn't love his neighbour cannot see God. Why not? Because he does not possess love. If he possessed love, he would see God, for "God is love".[162]

Who does not love other people, stays outside love and thus outside God for "God is love". . . . If instead of looking on people in a purely human fashion, you'd love them with spiritual love, you would see God who is love itself. You'd see him with an interior view which alone can make you see him.[163]

Augustine points out that we can know God precisely because we are aware of the love that exists in us. It is this experience itself: of our feelings towards others; our attempts to understand and reach out; our joy and excitement when making human contact; our desire to be honest and of use to others — in short: **The actual experience of our every-day "loving" is the reality in which we know God.** Let Augustine speak again.

Since we love other people through love, and "God is love", it is through God that we love them. We can only love by first loving love itself through which we give love. Therefore love of God and love of other people include each other.[164]

What?! Does it follow from the fact that you love love itself that you love God? Yes, definitely! By loving love, you love God. Have you forgotten what has been stated in Scripture: "God is love"? If "God is love", whoever loves love, loves God.[165]

Let no one say: I don't know what I love. Let him love his neighbour, then he will love love itself. In fact he will know the love with which he loves better than the people he loves. Therefore, God — who is love — will be better known to him than his neighbour; better known because God is more present; better known because God is more interior; better known because God is more certain.[166]

Without any doubt, if love lives in a person, he or she is a temple of God. For God is love.[167]

The Holy Spirit who is himself God, once given to a human person enkindles in that person love for God and for other people because the Spirit himself is love.[168]

How could God be more interior to us? Our human energy, our spirit, turns out to be nothing less than a manifestation of God's Spirit! Prompting us to a new level of loving, the Spirit of Jesus infuses new life in us. How can we respond to this?

How can we

more consciously live

the Love

that is God in us?

I will make some suggestions about this in the final chapter.

20

The Way
in to Love

It is not knowledge that opens the gates of heaven but love, as an ancient saying has it. Our world changes if we discover the central place of love. Through love nature looks different, relationships deepen, God becomes close, unexpected things can happen. Many new perspectives open up when we approach God as the source of love who is "within".

Perhaps there is no word in our language that carries as many associations in our mind as "love". At times its use is sloppy, sentimental, casual, if not tasteless. More often than not it strikes a tender chord in us. We may know from the care of our parents how unselfish love can be. We may have experienced the unspeakable thrill of "being in love", of having found a partner whose concern moves us, whose touch transforms us and whose intimate sharing frees us from the pain of loneliness. Perhaps we know real love in the form of strong and lasting friendships; the support our friends give us, their readiness to stand by us in time of trouble; their generosity in putting up with our failings, in not letting us down. Instinctively we know that such experiences of love are high points in our life — realities that afford most meaning and give us the greatest happiness.

I realize full well that our human relationships are based

on our innate need of "bonding" — a need articulated in millions of years of evolution. Our animal nature requires it. Parents and children bond. Man and wife bond. Members of the clan bond. Our chemistry, our psychology, our thinking are geared to bonding. The fact remains that love itself, which is based on such bonding and grows from it, goes much beyond it. We love not only a beautiful partner, but beauty as such. We love a true friend, but also truth in itself. As Plato pointed out more than two thousand years ago, human "eros" knows no limits. Its quest reaches out to infinity. It will never be fully satisfied with partial fulfilment. Is this not a remarkable finding — which we can verify in ourselves?

Where does this mighty impulse, this unquenchable thirst in us, come from? It can only be God. God is the irrepressible energy of being and life that caused the universe to explode at the Big Bang. That energy made space expand and matter evolve, until life erupted and intelligence was born. In the personality of every human individual it is God who puts the stamp of his uniqueness, his unrepeatability. In the search for happiness, in the joy of growth, in the intimacy of togetherness he creates the thrill, the satisfaction, the embrace.

The world in which we live is not a huge engine whose blueprint has been discovered by science. The world is much more mysterious; and it is full of divine love and purpose.

> Why should I a stranger be
> in my Father's dwelling,
> while hill and river, rock and tree
> of his love are telling?
> Always heard their simple voice
> bidding child-like hearts rejoice,
> whisper us his love is near.

> Joseph Gostick

171

The wonder of it all is that while nature follows its laws as unravelled by science, it carries a message that points beyond itself. Everything shows the face of God in some form or measure. The colours we see not only help us survive in a competitive world, they raise our mind to magnificence and splendour. When we admire the riotous glow of a rainbow or the soft hues of sapphire, purple and orange in a distant galaxy, do we not see beyond them the exuberant imagination that made them happen?

When we think about God, the source of all that exists, the Self from which we ourselves and the universe spring, words fall short, only images remain. Since we ourselves are persons, people who can know and love, we can meaningfully apply to God the image of "person". For even though his knowing and willing infinitely transcends ours, we know that he must possess these qualities *at least* to the degree in which we possess them. How otherwise could he shape our personality by imprinting his own likeness on us? How could he lack intelligence if he produces mind in us? How could he be without love, if his energy emerges as love in us? It is not enough, therefore, to think of him as an inanimate life force. We must give him a "face" in our thought. We can address him as a Father, a Mother, a Friend, as our deepest Self — remembering all the time that these are just human images expressing too little and saying it clumsily.

Our conscience is another way in which God, who is love, manifests his presence in us. Whether we like it or not, we know in our deepest self that right is right and wrong is wrong. We cannot, without destroying ourselves, go against the judgement of our own inner tribunal. The more sensitive we are to its dictates, and the more we shape our lives in conformity with truth and love, the happier we will be. We realize that this sense of responsibility again reflects in us the presence of a Person.

172

How could we feel guilty to a nameless life force? How could we feel rewarded if not by the approval of Someone who knows and cares? Does the response of our heart not prove our deep awareness of scrutiny by a Person — our Self about whose verdict we greatly care?

Prayer is something very personal. It cannot be tied down to specific practices or formulas. Prayer means no more than a conscious reaching out to the reality of God. There are times when our awareness of him is nurtured best by silence; by reflecting on ourselves, on nature, on events that happened. There are other times when it helps us to talk to God. This is not silly, even though our words will be so inadequate. Speaking is a natural human response. If we have never prayed in this fashion, we may need to cross the threshold by saying: "God, I'm searching for you". "God, make me know you're here." "God, help me to pray." "God, source of all love in me, I love you. I'm trying to love you." The words need not be beautiful, or long, or traditional. They should express what we feel. He will respond in his own way; unmistakably so if we learn to discern his working in our heart.

Having established contact with God, realizing that he is the source of love, other unexpected things may happen. We may suddenly find that certain aspects of life which baffle us — such as pain, sorrow, sickness, death — may have a meaning after all. Was evolution — in spite of its process of decays and new starts, of the survival of the fittest — the best way to make us become the autonomous persons we are now? Are pain and sorrow not tools to help us cope, rather than instruments of torture? Is our ability to sin not inherent in that greatest asset, our human freedom? If it is not health, prosperity and long life that are the highest values but love — are we missing out on a superior logic?

And what if God took the astounding initiative of

173

expressing his mind more directly to us? What if he began to communicate himself in unprecedented closeness? Who are we to call this unthinkable or absurd? I have explained how we Christians believe God has actually taken such a step through his special Image on earth, Jesus Christ. He told us that God *is* love. He poured into us a palpable measure of his Spirit of love. If this claim can be substantiated, as I believe it can, would it not confirm and specify what we already know of him from natural sources?

My words about God are like roads
running off
in all directions,
cleverly twined and knotted,
a network
spanning the land.
But just as well
they don't cover everything.
For flowers won't grow
on tarmac.

When sounds of a joyful song
  dance around me,
when the rhythm of rapture
  engulfs me,
it's music itself
  not the reviews
  not the scoresheet
that speaks to my heart.

Sparkling drops
  of fire in me
reveal your mystic
  melody.

NOTES

PREFACE. *Seeing God Upside Down*

1. J. Hessen, *Platonismus und Prophetismus,* Munich 1939; K.A.H. Hidding, *De Evolutie van het godsdienstig Bewustzijn,* Utrecht 1965.

2. J. Kerkhofs, *God in Europe,* Pro Mundi Vita, Brussels 1987.

CHAPTER 1 *Grandfather's Clock and Cosmic Alarm*

3. *Works of Philo Judaeus,* transl. C.D. Yonge, George Bell and Sons, London 1890, pp. 182-3.

CHAPTER 2 *Turtle-Shells and Deep Water*

4. *Tao Te Ching* 52,2.
5. More than forty translations exist of the TAO TE CHING. Among those I consulted are: L. Giles (Murray, London 1906); A. Waley (Macmillan, New York 1934); Lin Yutang (Modern Library, New York 1948); J.J.L. Duyvendak (Murray, London 1954); R.B. Blackney (Mentor, New York 1955); W. Chan (Bobbs-Merrill, Indianapolis 1963); D.C. Lau (Penguin, Harmondsworth 1963); G.F. Feng and J. English (Wildwood, London 1972).

6. The work of CHUANG TZU has been translated by: H.A. Giles, *Chuang Tzu* (Quaritch, London 1926); B. Watson, *The Complete Works of Chuang Tzu* (Columbia University Press, New York 1968); Y. Fung, *Chuang tzu* (Commercial Press, Shanghai 1933); T. Merton, *The Way of Chuang Tzu* (New Directions, New York 1969; selections only).

176

G.F. Feng and J. English, *Chuang Tsu: Inner Chapters* (Vintage, New York 1974).

7. *Chuang Tzu* 7,11; cf. T. Merton, op. cit., pp. 93-4.

8. Kuan Yin Tzu; quoted by D. Howard Smith, *The Wisdom of the Taoist Mystics,* Sheldon Press, London 1980, p. 60.

9. *I Ching,* The Great Appendix, section I, no. 72; see J. Legge, *I Ching, The Book of Changes,* Bantam, New York 1964, pp. 373-4.

10. *Chuang Tzu* 6,11.

11. Kuan Tzu, *P'ien* 49; compare A. Waley, *The Way and its Power,* Macmillan, New York 1934, p. 48.

CHAPTER 3 *The Creative Void of a Hunchback Tree*

12. *Chuang Tzu* 4,11.

13. *Chuang Tzu* 12,15.

14. *Chuang Tzu* 2,3.

15. *Chuang Tzu* 17,4.

16. *Tao Te Ching* 42,1.

17. *Tao Te Ching* 39,1.

18. *Chung Yung;* quoted by A. Watts, *Tao The Watercourse Way,* Penguin 1979, p. 37.

19. *Kuan Tzu;* cf. Waley, p. 49.

20. *Tao Te Ching* 1,1.

21. *Tao Te Ching* 14, 1-2.

22. *Tao Te Ching* 25,1.

23. Howard Smith p. 17.

24. *Chuang Tzu* 2,3.

25. *Chuang Tzu* 6,1.

26. *Chuang Tzu* 2,2.

27. *Chuang Tzu* 12,6.

28. *Chuang Tzu* 2,5.

29. *Tao Te Ching* 11.

CHAPTER 4 *Horizons Unknown to a Frog in a Well*

30. *Tao Te Ching* 32,2.

31. *Tao Te Ching* 34,1.

32. *Tao Te Ching* 8,1.

33. *Chuang Tzu* 17,1.

34. *Chuang Tzu ibidem.*

35. Rawson and Legge, p. 11.

36. *Chuang Tzu* 3,2.

37. *Chuang Tzu* 19,10.

38. *Tao Te Ching* 6.

39. *Tao Te Ching* 61,1.

40. *Tao Te Ching* 66,1.

41. *Tao Te Ching* 10; 15; 37; 48.

42. *Tao Te Ching* 37,1; 38,2; 48,2.

43. *Tao Te Ching* 27,1.

44. *Chuang Tzu* 13,1.

45. *Chuang Tzu* 6,7.

46. *Tao Te Ching* 78,1.

47. *Tao Te Ching* 43, 1-2

CHAPTER 5 *Faces Modelled Inside Out*

48. J. van Ruysbroeck, *Van den Geesteliken Tabernakel* ("About the Spiritual Tabernacle"), Kompas, Mechelen 1934, Vol. 2, p. 365. In this and *all* other quotes from Ruysbroeck I offer my own free translation of the original Flemish.

49. Ruysbroeck, *De Gheestelike Brulocht* ("The Spiritual Wedding"), Kompas, Mechelen 1932, Vol. 1, p. 148. Compare the English edition by E. Colledge, *The Spiritual Espousals,* New York 1953.

50. Ruysbroeck, *Een Spieghel der Eeuwigher Salicheit* ("Mirror of Eternal Beatitude"), Kompas, Mechelen 1934, Vol. 3, p. 166.

51. *Brulocht ibidem* (see note 49), pp. 203-4.

52. *Brulocht* ib. p. 203.

53. *Brulocht* ib. p. 145.

54. Ruysbroeck, *Van den Blinkenden Steen* ("About the Sparkling Stone"), Kompas, Mechelen 1934, Vol. 3, pp. 6-7.

55. Taken from Ruysbroeck's letters recently published in Dutch: *De Boodschap van Jan van Ruusbroec,* Lannoo, Tielt 1980. Among the little that has been published on Ruysbroeck in English, see: V. Scully, *A Mediaeval Mystic,* London 1910; J.H. Freeman, *John of Ruysbroeck,* Boston 1959.

CHAPTER 7 *Big Brother's Watchful Eye*

56. *Dies Irae* by Thomas of Celano, 13th century; transl. W.J. Irons, 1812-83.

57. Sura 20, 99-102, 111-13, my own free rendering based on the classic versions of J.M. Rodwell (Dent and Sons, London 1909), G. Parrinder and Abdullah Yusuf Ali (Islamic Foundation, Leicester 1975).

58. *Universal Islamic Declaration,* Islamic Council of Europe, London 1980, passim.

59. J.S. Moon, *Introduction to Islam,* H.M.I., Hyderabad 1981, p.37.

60. M. Tayyib Bakhsk, *A Short Handbook of Fiqh,* Kazi Publications, Lahore 1970, pp. 64-7; 76.

61. M. Pruemmer, *Manuale Theologiae Moralis,* Vol. 2, Herder, Freiburg 1936, pp. 390-9 (who, fortunately, rejects some of the worst legalist interpretations).

CHAPTER 8 *Layer upon Layer of Radiance*

62. A translation of this account, entitled *al-Mungid min ad-dalûl* ("The Deliverer from Error") can be found in *Anthology of Islamic Literature,* ed. J. Kritzeck, Penguin, Harmondsworth 1964, pp. 182-92.

63. For an introduction on Sufism, see I. Shah, *The Way of the Sufi,* Penguin, Harmondsworth 1974; L. Bakhtiar, *Sufi Expressions of the Mystic Quest,* Thames and Hudson, London 1976; R.E. Nicholson, *Studies in Islamic Mysticism,* Idarah, Delhi 1981; Ibn Ata'illah, *Sufi Aphorisms,* Suhail, Lahore 1985.

64. I will follow the translation by W.H.T. Gairdner, *Al-Ghazzali's Mishkat al-Anwar,* Kitab Bhavan, New Delhi 1981 (based on the Cairo edition of 1923).

65. The Arabic word Ghazali uses, *wajh,* means both "face" and "side", "aspect".

66. Ghazali, op. cit. (note 64) p. 59.

67. Ghazali, ibid. p. 63.

68. Ghazali, ibid. p. 66.

69. Muslim theologians derive this truth from a *hadith,* an oral tradition descending from Muhammad. Its real source, of course, is Genesis 1:27.

70. Ghazali, op. cit. p. 49.

71. Ghazali, op. cit. p. 60.

72. Ghazali, op. cit. p. 86.

73. Ghazali, op. cit. pp. 75-6.

74. Ghazali, op. cit. pp. 60-1.

75. *Shorter Encyclopaedia of Islam,* ed. H. Gibb and J. Kramer, Brill, Leiden 1953, under *tassawwuf,* p. 580.

76. I. Shah, *The Way of the Sufi,* Penguin 1974, p. 268. I have modernized the

translation.

CHAPTER 9 *The Ant, the Stone and the Pitchdark Night*

77. See I. Shah, *The Way of the Sufi,* Penguin 1974, p. 113 (rendering my own).

78. I. Shah, ib. p. 87.

79. I. Shah, ib. p. 242.

80. *Encyclopaedia of Islam,* Brill, Leiden 1971, Vol. 13, under *Halladj,* pp. 99-104.

81. E. Schroeder, extract from *Akhbar al-Hallaj,* in *Anthology of Islamic Literature,* Penguin 1964, pp. 104-13; esp. p. 108.

82. I. Shah, ib. p. 197.

83. *Shorter Encyclopaedia of Islam,* Brill, Leiden 1953, p. 580.

84. Al-Ghazali, *Mishkat al-Anwar,* ed. W.H. Gairdner, Kitab Bhavan, New Delhi 1981, pp. 75-7.

85. Al-Ghazali, ibid. p. 63.

86. Al-Ghazali, ibid. p. 52.

87. Al-Ghazali, ibid. p. 46.

88. Al-Ghazali, ibid. p. 47-51.

89. I. Shah, op. cit. p. 112.

90. I. Shah, ibid. p. 137.

91. Al-Ghazali, *Faysal al-tafriqa bayn al-Islam wa l-zandaqa,* ed. Cairo 1901, p.75; see J. Wijngaards, "I call you to Salvation" (Qur 40, 44), *Indian Ecclesiastical Studies* 9 (1970) 247-50.

92. I. Shah, ibid. p. 275.

93. I. Shah, ibid. p. 297.

94. I. Shah, ibid. p. 180.

CHAPTER 10 *The Mirror and the Lens Inside Us*

95. J.H. Newman, *An Essay in Aid of a Grammar of Assent,* Longmans, London 1870, pp. 101-17.

96. J.H. Newman, *Callista,* London 1870, p. 314.

97. *The Church in the Modern World* No. 16; cf. A. Flannery, *Vatican Council II,* Dominican Publications, Dublin 1975, p. 916 (inclusive language my own).

98. *Declaration on Religious Liberty* No. 3; cf. Flannery, ib. pp. 801-2.

99. Regarding Paul's teaching, see especially: J. Lecuyer, "Pentecôte et loi nouvelle", *La Vie Spirituelle* 25 (1953) 471-90; S. Lyonnet, "St Paul: Liberty and Law", *The Bridge* 4 (1962) 229-51.

100. Thomas Aquinas, *Summa*

Theologica, Pars Prima Secundae, Q. 106, art 1; ed. De Rubeis, Marrietti, Turin 1932, Vol. 2, p. 648 (translation my own).

101. *In Hebraeos* cap 8, lect. 1; *In 2 Corinthios* cap. 3, lect. 2; cf. S. Lyonnet, op. cit. (note 99), pp. 8-9.

102. *Summa Theologica,* ib. Q. 106, art 2.

103. Ghazali, *Miskat al-Anwar,* ib. p. 56.

CHAPTER 12   *Sparks from the Mind's Furnace*

104. It was the atheist A. Compte who first identified the three different stages in human thinking, which he called "mythological, metaphysical and positivist", in *The Catechism of Positivist Religion,* Trubner, London 1883. C.A. Van Peursen corrected and refined the notion, calling the three stages "mythological, metaphysical and functional" in: "Man and Reality. The History of Human Thought", *The Student World,* Vol. 56, 1963. H. Cox worked it out more fully in *The Secular City. Secularization and Urbanization in Theological Perspective,* Penguin 1968.

105. *Rigveda* III, 18.

106. Lucretius, *On the Nature of the Universe,* passim in I 483-704. An English translation of the whole book was made by R.E. Latham, Penguin 1951.

107. *Rigveda* I, 1.1.

CHAPTER 13   *The Power Perception of Ancient Myths*

108. A readable and attractive account of the oldest human societies can be found in: F. Clark Howell, *Early Man,* Time-Life International 1970. Other good background books are: G. Childe, *What Happened in History?,* Penguin 1957; W.E. Le Gros Clark, *History of the Primates,* British Museum London (also in paperback); T.H. Huxley, *Man's Place in Nature,* University of Michigan Press, Cresset 1950 (also in paperback); D. Morris, *The Naked Ape,* Corgi, London 1968.

109. Among anthropological works on primitive societies we can

recommend: A. Goldenweiser, *Anthropology: An Introduction to Primitive Culture,* London 1937; E. Durkheim, *Elementary Forms of Religious Life,* London 1926; B. Malinowski, *Magic, Science and Religion,* Boston Press 1948.

110. On the specific topic of the earliest ideas of the "divine" the following books are considered classics: E. Cassirer, *Language and Myth,* Dover Publications 1946; J. Frazer, *The Golden Bough,* Macmillan, New York, 1924; A.R. Radcliffe-Brown, *Tabu,* Cambridge 1940; M. Eliade, *Patterns in Comparative Religion,* Sheed and Ward, London 1958.

111. See P. Maranda (Ed), *Mythology: Selected Readings,* Education Penguin 1972, for the best compact introduction to authors and opinions on myth. Two earlier collections are also very informative: T. A. Sebeok (Ed), *Myth: A Symposium,* Indiana University Press 1958 (also in paperback); J. Middleton (Ed), *Myth and Cosmos: Readings in Mythology and Symbolism,*

American Museum of Natural History 1967.

112. C. Levi-Strauss has been one of the recognized authorities on primitive myth-making. I recommend: *The Savage Mind,* University of Chicago Press 1966; *The Raw and the Cooked,* Harper and Row 1969.

113. On the characteristics and origin of the oldest religious beliefs information can be had from: P. Radin, *Primitive Religion,* Hamish Hamilton, London 1938; J. Maringer, *The Gods of Prehistoric Man,* Weidenfeld and Nicholson, London 1960; E.O. James *Prehistoric Religion,* Barnes and Noble, 1961 (also in paperback).

114. Comparative religion is the science that collects and analyses data from religions that exist or that have existed. A.C. Bouquet, *Comparative Religion,* Penguin 1941, updated 1967, provides a good survey of the results obtained. A systematic observation of religions is given by G. Van der Leeuw, *Religion in Essence and Manifestation,* George

182

Allen and Unwin, London 1938.

115. The most influential writer on the psychology of religious belief at the beginning of this century was W. James. His books are still widely read in paperback reprints: *The Will to Believe*, Dover Publications, New York 1956; *The Varieties of Religious Experience*, Fontana/Fount 1960. Other leading psychological authors who ascribe belief in God to the immaturity of primitive people: S. Freud, *The Future of an Illusion*, Hogarth, London 1949; E. Fromm, *Psychoanalysis and Religion*, Yale, New Haven 1950; M. Murray, *The Genesis of Religion*, Routledge and Kegan Paul, London 1963.

116. A thought-provoking discussion on mythological thinking in Christianity is offered in: J.A.T. Robinson, *Honest to God*, SCM, London 1963; D.L. Edwards (Ed), *The Honest to God Debate*, SCM, London 1963. Robinson presents his own, more matured ideas in *The Human Face of God*, SCM, London 1972.

117. S. Radhakrishnan, *The Idealist View of Life*, Penguin, London 1961, pp. 138-9.

118. S. Radhakrishnan develops the idea of the "integral experience" of God in many publications. Available with Allen and Unwin are: *Indian Philosophy; An Idealist View of Life; East and West in Religion; The Hindu View of Life; Recovery of Faith;* etc. Read also: J.G. Arapura, *Radhakrishnan and Integral Experience*, Asia Publishing House, Calcutta 1966.

119. The nineteenth century counted quite a few European exponents of the approach to God through the "numinous". Principal works of that time have been reprinted: R. Otto, *The Idea of the Holy*, Oxford University Press, London 1923; A.E. Taylor, *Does God Exist?*, Macmillan and Co., London 1945: excerpt in J. Hick (Ed.), *The Existence of God*, Macmillan, New York 1964, pp. 153-64. Modern forms of the intuitive grasp of God are defended by J. Maritain, *Approaches to God*, Harper and Row, New York 1954;

J. Baillie, *Our Knowledge of God*, Oxford University Press, London 1937; *The Sense of the Presence of God*, Oxford University Press, London 1963; H.D. Lewis, *Our Experience of God*, Allen and Unwin, London 1959.

CHAPTER 14   *Deep but Dry-as-Dust Deductions*

120. For the growth of a typical city 10,000–2,000 B.C. read: J. Garstang and J.B.E. Garstang, *The Story of Jericho*, London 1948; K.M. Kenyon, *Excavations at Jericho*, London 1960.

121. A good introduction to the Harappa culture in the Indus Valley and the philosophy to which it gave rise, is provided by A.L. Basham, *The Wonder that was India*, Orient Longmans, Calcutta 1963. See also: D.D. Kosambi, *The Culture and Civilization of Ancient India in Historical Outline*, Routledge and Kegan Paul, London 1965.

122. The birth of metaphysical thinking is best documented in the case of Greek philosophy. History books and introductions to Greek philosophy should be studied side by side. I recommend: C.M. Bowra, *Classical Greece*, Time-Life International 1966; J.C. Stobart, *The Glory that was Greece*, Nicholls, Four-Star Paperback, London 1962; F. Copleston, *A History of Philosophy, Vol. 1, Part 1, Greek Philosophy*, Doubleday paperback, New York 1962; F.M. Cornford, *Before and after Socrates*, Cambridge University Press 1968.

123. Aristotle's *Metaphysics* has been published in English by J. Warrington, Dent and Sons, London 1956. Read also: G.E.R. Lloyd, *Aristotle. The Growth and Structure of his Thought*, Cambridge University Press 1968.

124. Works of Philo Judaeus, transl. C.D. Yonge, George Bell and Sons, London 1890; also in C.H. Hartshorne and W.L. Reese, *Philosophers Speak of God*, University of Chicago Press, Chicago 1953, p. 77.

125. The discussion between Dharmakirthi and Trilocana has been described by G. Oberhammer in three

184

articles: *Wiener Zeitschrift f.d.K.S.O.A.* 8 (1964) 131-81; *Numen* 12 (1965) 1-34; *Zeitschrift für Katholische Theologie* 89 (1967) 446-57.

126. *The Upanishads,* transl. by F.M. Mueller in 1879; Dover Publications, New York 1980.

127. The arguments of Thomas Aquinas can be found in: *Summa Contra Gentiles* I, ch. 12-13; III, ch. 29; *Summa Theologica* I. q.2. a. 2-3. J.F. Anderson brought out an English translation of the *Contra Gentiles* as *On the Truth of the Catholic Faith,* Doubleday paperback in six volumes, 1956. Discussion on St Thomas's arguments in: J.F. Anderson, *Natural Theology,* Bruce, Milwaukee 1961; R.L. Patterson, *The Conception of God in the Philosophy of Aquinas,* Allen and Unwin, London 1933; E.G. Jay, *The Existence of God,* SPCK, London 1949.

128. *A Reader on Islam,* ed. A. Jeffrey, Mouton, The Hague 1962, pp. 356-7.

129. For a variety of presentations of the traditional arguments, the following books will be helpful: R. Garrigou Lagrange, *God: His Existence and His Nature,* Herder, St Louis 1914: E.L. Mascall, *He Who Is,* Longmans and Green, London 1943; Id., *Existence and Analogy,* Longmans and Green, London 1949; M. Pontifex, *The Existence of God,* Longmans, London 1946; R. Jolivet, *The God of Reason,* Burns and Oates, Faith and Facts No. 15, London 1956.

CHAPTER 15   *The Search for a Phantom Gardener*

130. My own version. An English translation of Anselm's *De Veritate* was published by R. McKeon, in *Selections from Medieval Philosophers,* Vol. 1, Charles Scribner's, New York 1929. Excerpts are found in C.H. Hartshorne and W.I. Reese (Ed.), *Philosophers Speak of God,* University of Chicago Press, 1953, pp. 96-106 (with introduction and comment). In *The Existence of God,* Macmillan, London 1964 (p.b.), pp. 23-47, J. Hick (Ed.) published side by side all the classical texts related to the ontological argument:

excerpts from Anselm, Descartes and Leibnitz in its favour; the arguments of Aquinas, Kant and Malcolm against it.

131. K. Barth has revived Anselm's argument in a strictly theological understanding: *Anselm: Fides Quaerens Intellectum*, SCM, London 1931. A thorough discussion of the original argument and its interpretation in: E. Gilson, *God and Philosophy*, Yale University Press, New Haven 1941; H. Bouillard, *The Knowledge of God*, Burns and Oates, London 1969.

132. The following works are representative of the Kantian stand: I. Kant, *Critique of Pure Reason and Dialogues Concerning Natural Religion*, by N.K. Smith (Ed.), Oxford 1935; J. Laird, *Theism and Cosmology*, Allen and Unwin, London 1940; A.J. Ayer, *Language, Truth and Logic*, Gollancz, London 1946.

133. The Thomists have replied in publications such as these: H.S. Box, *The World and God*, SPCK, London 1934; *God and the Modern*

Mind, SPCK, London 1937; R.P. Philips, *Modern Thomistic Philosophy*, Burns and Oates, London 1935; H. de Lubac, *The Drama of Atheistic Humanism*, Sheed and Ward, London 1949; Id., *The Discovery of God*, Darton, Longman and Todd, London 1960; C.A. Coulson, *Science and Christian Belief*, Oxford University Press, 1955 (also in p.b.).

134. B. Russell, *History of Western Philosophy*, Allen and Unwin, London 1946; Id., *Why I am not a Christian*, Allen and Unwin, London 1957.

135. E. A. Sillem, *George Berkeley and the Proofs of the Existence of God*, Longmans and Green, London 1957; Id., *Ways of Thinking about God, Thomas Aquinas and some recent problems*, Darton, Longman and Todd, London 1961; D. Jenkins, *The Christian Belief in God*, Faber and Faber, London 1964.

136. A Flew (Ed.), *Logic and Language*, Blackwell, Oxford 1955; Id., *God and Philosophy*, Hutchinson, London 1966; A. Flew and A. MacIntyre (Ed.), *New*

186

Essays in Philosophical Theology, SCM, London 1955; H.J. Paton, *The Modern Predicament,* Allen and Unwin, London 1955; A. MacIntyre, *Difficulties in Christian Belief,* SCM, London 1959.

137. V. Gordon Childe, *Man makes Himself,* Mentor Paperback, New York 1951.

138. T. de Chardin, *Hymn of the Universe* (1964), *The Phenomenon of Man* (1965) and *The Future of Man* (1969), all with Fontana/Fount, London.

CHAPTER 16   *Prayer in the Stock Exchange*

139. The features of today's city life are described in: P.K. Hatt and A.J. Reiss (Ed.). *Cities and Society,* Free Press, New York 1957; N. Anderson, *The Urban Community: A World Perspective,* Holt, Rinehart and Winston, New York 1959; E. Mayo *The Social Problems of an Industrial Civilization,* Routledge and Kegan Paul, London 1959; C.F. Stover, *The Technological Order,* Wayne State University Press, Detroit 1963; T. Burns (Ed.), *Industrial Man,*

Penguin 1969.

140. On the consequences of urbanization for Christianity: P. Albrecht, *The Churches and Rapid Social Change,* Doubleday, New York 1961; G. Winter, *The New Creation as Metropolis,* Macmillan, New York 1963; P. van Buren, *Theological Explorations,* SCM, London 1968. See also the works of Van Peursen and Cox mentioned in note 104.

141. L. Wittgenstein was the first to distinguish "language games" clearly. Read esp. his *Philosophical Investigations,* Blackwell, Oxford 1968. Other good introductions: J.L. Austin, *How to do things with words,* Oxford University Press, London 1970; J.R. Searle (Ed.), *The Philosophy of Language,* Oxford University Press 1971.

142. For "God-talk" explained as ethics, see R.B. Braithwaite, *An Empiricist's View of the Nature of Religious Belief,* Cambridge University Press, 1955. A more acceptable presentation of it as the "language of parable" is given by T.R. Miles in

Religion and the Scientific Outlook, Allen and Unwin, London 1969.

143. Meta-communication and its implications for belief in God are explained by P. Watzlawick et al., *Pragmatics of Human Communications,* Norton, New York 1970.

144. A good theological discussion of the linguistics of "God-talk" has been provided by I. Ramsey in *Religious Language,* SCM, London 1957; *Christian Discourse,* Oxford University Press, London 1965.

145. P. Davies sketches the new developments in *God and the New Physics,* Penguin 1984. A much more daring integration is proposed by F. Capra, *The Tao of Physics,* Fontana, London 1976 (updated edition in 1983); F.A. Wolf, *Taking the Quantum Leap,* Harper and Row, San Francisco 1980.

CHAPTER 17   *The Way in to "Grasping" God*

146. Thomas Aquinas, *De potentia* VII, 5, ad 14; see also *In Boetiae de Trinitate,* 7, 2, ad 1.

147. Ruysbroeck, *The Book of the Twelve Beguines,* B.II, 3-4; in *Werken,* Het Kompas, Mechelen 1932, pp. 21-2.

148. The text is from the so-called Pseudo-Dennis The Areopagite, *Mystical Theology,* ch. 4 and 5. I made my own free translation of it and rearranged the order of the paragraphs slightly. For the original, see "Sancti Dionysii Areopagitae", *Opera Omnia,* ed. B. Corderius, Zatta, Venice 1755, pp. 543-88.

CHAPTER 18   *He Pitches His Tent next door to Us*

149. E. Levinas, *Totality and Infinity,* Duquesne University Press, Pittsburgh 1969.

150. E.H. Erikson, *Identity,* New York 1968, pp. 96-100.

151. H. Faber, "Wisselende Patronen van religieuze ervaring", *Tijdschrift voor Theologie* 11 (1971) 225-48; A. Hardy, *The Spiritual Nature of Man,* Clarendon Press, Oxford 1979, pp. 134-6.

152. Obviously the two parents

exercise both a mother and a father function. I retain the exclusive formulation for clarity's sake.

153. The concept of the "I-Thou" in a religious context has been worked out well by M. Buber, *I and Thou,* T. and T. Clark, Edinburgh 1937; "The Eclipse of God", in *Religion and Ethics,* Harper and Row, New York 1951.

154. J. Wijngaards, *Jesus For Ever. Facts and Faith,* Catholic Truth Society, London 1987.

CHAPTER 19 *His Spirit Flows in Our Veins*

155. Plato, *Symposion,* Prisma edition, Utrecht 1960.

156. M. Scheler, *Vom Ewigen im Menschen,* Cologne 1921; *Die Stellung der Menschen im Kosmos,* Berlin 1928.

157. W. Pannenberg, "The Question of God", in *Basic Questions in Theology,* Vol. 2, Philadelphia 1971, pp. 216-27.

158. M. Blondel, *L'Action,* Paris 1893; K. Rahner, *Spirit in the World,* London 1968; B. Lonergan, *Method in Theology,* London 1972, pp.10, 105-11.

159. J. Wijngaards, *Experiencing Jesus,* Ave Maria Press, Notre Dame 1981, esp. pp. 9-28.

160. Augustine, *Treatise on St John's Letters* 8, 12.

161. Ibidem 5, 7.

162. Ibidem 9, 10.

163. Augustine, *About the Trinity* 8, 12.

164. Ibidem 8, 12.

165. *Treatise on St John's letters* 9, 10.

166. *About the Trinity* 8, 12.

167. *Sermons* 350, 1.

168. *About the Trinity* 15, 31. For a full exposition of Augustine's teaching on love I recommend: D. Dideberg, "Esprit Saint et charité", *Nouvelle Revue Théologique* 97 (1975) 97-109; 229-50; and, by the same author, *Augustine et la première Epître de Saint Jean,* Beauchesne, Paris 1976.